Pilgrim's
Process

Gerald J. Jud

Pilgrim's Process

*How the Local Church Can Respond
to the New Age*

 **United Church Press**
Philadelphia ~ Boston

Illustrations

Library of Congress Catalog Card Number 67-21651
Printed in the United States of America

TO MY WIFE, ELISABETH,

AND TO

OUR FELLOW PILGRIMS

CAROL, DANIEL, AND VIRGINIA

Preface

THIS IS A BOOK about the local church. It is written especially for those who are members of its core group.

Every local church has a core group. It is made up of persons who love the church, who bear the heaviest burdens in seeing that the institution is kept alive. They worry most about it. They are present regularly for worship, provide financial support, teach church school, serve on boards and committees, are deacons and trustees. They are instrumental in the coming and going of clergy.

Because these core members invest so much of themselves in the local church, they have deep feelings about the church and are sensitive to the storms now sweeping it because of the changes taking place in world and church. It is this group that will determine whether or not a church will make creative response to the new time now struggling to be born.

If you are a member of such a core group, this book is for you. It is a book for insiders. It is written with the prayer that it will make you thoughtful about the church you love and that it will help you help your church move beyond restlessness to creativity.

The title of this book brings together a very old term and a very new one. The old word, *pilgrim,* designates those who are consciously on a journey of faith, specifically here as members of the local church today. Such continue the story of the pilgrim people of God in the Old and New Testaments. *Process,* the new word, points to the way of getting from here to there. The feel of this concept is action, motion, procedure, forward movement, progress, and change. The word signals not a static way of life but a dynamic life-style. Put the two words together and the intention of this book comes clear: to show the pilgrim style as appropriate for the church in these changing times, and to show that implicit in this style is the process through which the church may make faithful response to her Lord as Lord of the new age.

The 1961 meeting of the World Council of Churches at New Delhi authorized a long-range study on "The Missionary Structure of the Congregation." This study has proceeded on the basis of working groups of biblical scholars, theologians, pastors, church administrators, and sociologists. Groups have been at work in North America, East Germany, Western Europe, Southeast Asia, and South America. The Western European group has made its full report, and the North American section has reported on its first stage. Both these reports are now available in a single volume. I have participated in this study, and this exciting venture has strongly influenced my thinking. The emerging theological consensus is reflected in this book.

I would like to acknowledge my indebtedness particularly to the colleagues with whom I have been engaged in this study: Hans Hoekendijk, professor of missions, Union Theological Seminary, New York; Colin Williams, associate general secretary of the Division of Christian Life and Mission, National Council of Churches; Harvey Cox, assistant professor of theology and culture at Harvard University Divinity School; Hans J. Margull, professor of missions, University of Hamburg, West Germany; Thomas

Wieser of the Division of Christian Life and Mission, National Council of Churches; and Gabriel Fackre, professor of theology and culture, Lancaster Theological Seminary.

Deep appreciation goes also to my colleague Willis E. Elliott, whose busy red pencil and probing mind have influenced this manuscript in important ways.

Portions of this book were given as *The Jesse M. Bader Lectures in Christian Evangelism*. They were presented at The Divinity School of Drake University, Des Moines, Iowa, April 26 and 27, 1967. Lr. Bader, a minister of The World Convention of the Churches of Christ (Disciples), had a long and distinguished career as the secretary of evangelism for the Federal Council of Churches and later the National Council of Churches.

Contents

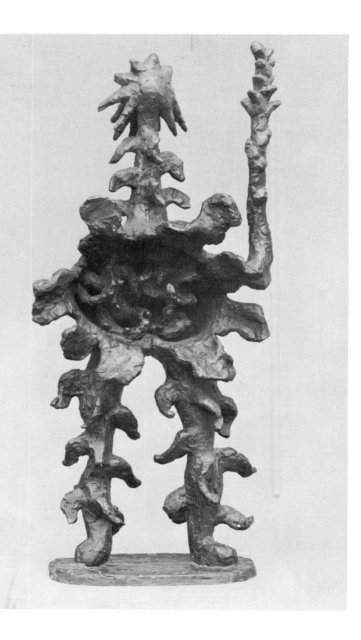

Introduction

THINGS ARE ALL STIRRED UP in the local church that I belong to in suburban New York. Our pastor is convinced that our age is so new that the church needs to busy itself with updating its message, methods, structure, and style. He calls himself something of a cliff-hanger and is very honest in sharing both his doubts and his hopes with his people. His sermons are never dull, although they are often disturbing because he himself is so obviously on pilgrimage and is so bent on encouraging others to be on theirs.

When I say that things are stirred up in our local church, that is just what I mean. Some people have left. As they leave, many of these say that they don't want to be stirred up in church—helped and comforted, yes; stirred up, no. Others are not very happy but, refusing to think that things must always go their way, they hang on uncomplainingly. Some of these just don't care enough to protest loudly; others have high hopes that the present incumbent will soon receive the second tea and leave; and still others are quietly open-minded in spite of their discontentment.

Like their pastor, many in this church are cliff-hangers. They are glad when Sunday rolls around, and they carry on a very active dialogue with the troubled who express their anguish but do not leave the church. Many in this latter group are wide open to dialogue. They respect an honest man who shows himself unafraid of controversy and who

13

does not muffle his message because of fear of losing his job. So study groups have sprung up like toadstools, and in homes and parties the discussion is often on the crisis of the church. A form-and-mission committee has been appointed to isolate the issues, study them, and report ways of creatively addressing the crisis of the church.

Last Laity Sunday two of our laymen carried on a dialogue in the chancel. They had been carefully selected to represent different poles in the dialogue going on within the whole church. Their presentations were authentic and revealing. So precisely do they point up the crucial issues that I could think of no better way to engage you in the message of this book than to let you read their full discourse. As you read their remarks and answers to the questions, surface your own responses. You and the people of your church are responsible for forging responses to these questions.

MR. NETHERCUT:

This church needs members who have the guts and the imagination to turn everything upside down. And it needs other members to keep them from turning upside down those things that ought to be rightside up. Above all, it needs members who are willing to talk to one another about their differences, challenge one another's viewpoints, yield or hold fast with equal grace, and, through it all, continue to respect one another as honest and sincere men and as fellow church members.

This morning Ferol Overfelt and I will discuss a few sharply focused questions. We have consciously chosen questions on which we have somewhat different viewpoints. We hope that these differences will stimulate you to think through your own answers. We hope also that you will recognize that there are many, many matters on which we have no major difference in viewpoint. Both of us recognize and cherish the vital role this church has had in our own lives. We recognize that Christianity is a joyful and challenging adventure, not a verbal tug-of-war. We share the hope and faith that God will find this church acceptable for his purposes in our community. We agree that it is not enough simply to have a tender feeling about the Christian way.

What the church needs, and needs badly, is some tough-minded thinking about *what the Christian today really believes and what such beliefs demand of him and of this church.* We need to face up to troubling questions that have no easy answers. Ferol and I have selected three of these for our comments this morning. The first is this: *Should the primary concern of our church be the needs of our members and their families or the needs of outsiders?* Ferol, how would you answer that question?

MR. OVERFELT:

Phil, with respect to this question I have the conviction that the *primary concern of our church should be to meet the needs of its members and their families* before attempting to go too far afield. What are some of these needs? I think all of us need and look forward to attending meaningful church services every Sunday as God commanded in Deuteronomy 5:12. We need the lift and inspiration given to us by good church music and challenging sermons and prayers. Although we should be proud of the services now being held, all concerned should keep them under constant evaluation in the endeavor to inspire and retain our present members and to attract new members.

Many of our members require additional activity other than attending church services once a week to meet their obligations as faithful Christians. Our church attempts to meet this need by providing opportunities for worthwhile service on its many boards and committees, its fine choirs, its Women's Guild, and its Men's Fellowship. Here again, it is important that the activities of these groups be constantly appraised for maximum effectiveness. Furthermore, our adult members who are fortunate to have children place great importance on the Christian upbringing and training of their youngsters. Although all of them undoubtedly recognize that much of this training must be given in the home, these parents require effective Christian education for their children in a well-planned and organized church school. This they are getting in our church today; and, here again, adult members of our church have another opportunity to render Christian service by serving on the staff of our church school.

It seems obvious to me that *our church can be more effective in*

15

meeting these needs of its members than it can in trying to meet the needs of outsiders because it has complete control over its services, its miscellaneous boards, committees, and groups, and its program of Christian education. In my judgment, it seems reasonable that the members of our church will be *stronger* Christians and more willing to help meet the needs of outsiders if their own needs are fulfilled through effective local programs.

MR. NETHERCUT:

It is very difficult to argue against serving the people who are nearest and dearest to us. It is tempting to be conciliatory by saying that serving our own needs and serving the needs of others are not mutually exclusive goals. But certainly these are not identical goals. Which is to come *first?* Which is our primary concern?

In Matthew 25, there is no question about which comes first. Serving our own needs isn't even considered. The only issue, the only criterion for judgment, is how well we serve the least of God's brethren—the hungry, the naked, the sick—how well we minister to their needs, not to our own needs.

There are several ways we can react to that parable. One is to say, "All right, you've found a parable that says we must serve the needy, not ourselves; certainly there must be other passages in the Bible that say we should serve our loved ones first, before we go too far afield." I invite you to search for such a passage. You may find it, but I couldn't.

Does this mean we shouldn't serve our loved ones and help our friends? No, of course we should love and serve them, but there is a higher demand that God places on us—that we love and serve people who are not our own people but who are God's people and who need help, and whose needs are vastly greater than our own.

But, some of us may say, we must be practical about this. We can't really help others outside of our church unless and until we have a strong membership. The way we get a strong membership is to satisfy our own needs first. Then perhaps we'll be able to help others.

As Americans, we pride ourselves on being practical. We pride ourselves on the strength of our church, on using the same kind of practical yardsticks that we use to evaluate our businesses, rate our television shows, or judge the progress of our children in school. We believe that we're making a "go of things" in our church if

16

the membership is growing, the services are well attended, the physical plant is well maintained, and our programs are satisfying to our members. All of these may indeed be gratifying to us, but Matthew 25 is a jarring reminder that God doesn't judge us on our practicality or on our so-called strength or on the degree to which our church members are satisfied. He asks only, "How did you serve the least of these my brethren?" And we must ask ourselves: Do we have the courage and the humility to measure ourselves and our church by that yardstick? Do we have the courage and the faithfulness to make the least of our brethren our primary concern?

The second question Ferol and I have selected is really two questions: *In today's world what are the appropriate areas of church concern, and how do we as a church act on these concerns?*

I answer the first of those two questions by saying simply that there are no areas which are inappropriate for church concern. Our political, social, and economic problems are as properly matters of church concern as they are of the political party, the social agency, and the business enterprise. We cannot polarize God's world into the religious versus the secular, or the proper ecclesiastical concerns versus the so-called improper worldly concerns of God's church, as if there could be any part of human activity about which God is not concerned.

But the second part of the question is more controversial. How do we as a church act on these concerns? At the risk of sounding flippant, an honest answer to the question "How do we as a church act?" would be "Only very rarely." In too many cases Christianity has become a vast spectator sport. Members come to church to be inspired, to compare the performances of ministers and the choirs, to hear about the latest books of the new theologians, and to rejoice vicariously in the work of dedicated laity and ministers serving in remote areas. All too frequently, as a church we stop short of the only step that really counts—following such inspiration and such example with meaningful church action.

Since it is obviously difficult for the church to act as a corporate body, it is heartening to see new action groups taking shape in the Youth Fellowship, in the Women's Guild, and in completely informal groups which are open to all individuals who are interested in serving the needs of the world through our church. They should be strongly encouraged to use this church as a rallying point for their concern and their actions. To do so may distress and even enrage those church members who fear that any group action may be construed as representing the action of the entire church. But for church members to be blocked as they attempt to use the church as a channel for serving God's world raises the troublesome questions: Whom really are we trying to please? Whom really are we trying to obey?

Ferol, are there other ways in which we can act as a church?

MR. OVERFELT:

Phil, any good Christian must agree that ideally there are no inappropriate areas of church concern, be they political, social, economic, domestic, or foreign. I feel, however, that it is most difficult, if not impossible, for our church as a body to take any effective action with respect to most of the world's burning questions of the day. What can we do as a church about the war in Vietnam, apartheid in South Africa, famine in India, and low living standards in the have-not countries of the world? Getting closer to home, what effective action, if any action, can we take to improve racial imbalance in this country, to increase employment of blue-collar workers, to clean up the ghettos of Detroit, Chicago, and Los Angeles? And still closer, can we help to improve the living conditions of Negroes in New York City and White Plains, the pollution of waters of the Hudson River and Long Island Sound, the building of a new village hall, and the widening and straightening of the Bronx River Parkway?

Probably we might be expected to participate in the solution, or improvement, of situations in Scarsdale, in Westchester County, in New York City, and in our state more actively and effectively than we could in problems farther afield. *But what officials, or what groups, within our church decide the matters of church concern that deserve our attention?* And once decided, how do we proceed? Under our present organization, once decided, the matter would undoubtedly be referred to the appropriate board or committee for action, and that board or committee would act in the name of the church, since our membership as a whole does not usually pass on such matters. In purely local matters perhaps some action could be taken without incurring any monetary cost, but generally action in most areas would necessitate some expenditure of funds. And money is an item in short supply with our church. This shortage alone greatly limits the areas in which we can take effective action. Assuming we have the funds, action in national and/or international matters could be best achieved by working through larger bodies in which we have confidence, such as the parent United Church of Christ, the World Council of Churches, the American Red Cross, and similar organizations.

That such organizations are actively concerned with present-day problems was evidenced in meetings of the World Council of Churches, an organization of more than two hundred Protestant and Orthodox denominations, in Geneva this summer. Billed as the most important meeting on social issues ever held by the eighteen-year-old organization, the council denounced U.S. participation in Vietnam, urged that Communist China be brought into the United Nations, condemned nuclear war as "the greatest of evils," denounced the white-supremacy regime of Ian Smith in Rhodesia, and concluded that "participation in political life is a valid form of ministry." Evangelist Billy Graham, in opposing such radical or revolutionary positions, holds that the error of many churchmen in trying to cure the ills of society lies in their approaching the task as if society were already made up of "truly Christian men." Dr. Graham believes that *the changing of men is the primary mission of the church* and that "the only way to change men is to get them converted to Jesus Christ; then they will have the capacity to live up to the Christian command: Love thy neighbor." It is this mission that I advocate for our church in Scarsdale.

Now I turn to the question, what am I to do as an individual Christian? Each individual must determine for himself where and how he feels God wants him to be at work. There can be little argument against the position that a faithful Christian should support his church to the full extent of his ability—by attending worship services regularly, by making financial contributions, by willingly serving on boards and committees, and by loyally supporting his church generally.

Beyond his personal participation in church affairs, a good Christian will practice his Christianity in all of his personal and business affairs. He will not reserve it for special occasions, but will act as he thinks God would have him act in his relationships with members of his family, his neighbors, his social and business associates, and with strangers. He should take an active interest in affairs, local, national, and international, and, to the best of his abil-

19

ity and resources, participate in and contribute to those causes he believes in most.

MR. NETHERCUT:

Ferol has outlined the opportunities we have for demonstrating in our individual lives what it means to be a Christian. I would like to comment on two temptations that arise from these opportunities, two temptations each of us must face as an individual.

First, the size and complexity of the world's needs make it tempting for us to say there's really nothing an individual can do. Nothing? This is a common mistake, for there isn't a world problem that does not begin right where we are, and always we can diminish or add to it. We can be a part of the problem or a part of the solution. Not to be aware of this, not to know the difference one person can make, is in itself one of the world problems.

Consider the major problems of our times—ignorance, poverty, oppression, hatred. We don't need to look far to find them. There are ignorant, poor, oppressed, and hate-filled people just beyond the walls of our church and just beyond the walls we build in our imagination around our community. Many of these people can't be reached by the institutional church or by any other institution. They can be reached and helped only if we go as individuals to them as individuals. When we do that, when we venture out beyond our walls, we reduce the world's problems right where we are.

It is not easy to do this. The status quo has been good to us. One reason we came to Scarsdale was to get away from these problems. But we have no right to get away. We have no right to be indifferent. The divine right of the successful is as false a notion as the divine right of kings. If our idea of Christianity is only to live decently and not to add further to the injustices of the world, we are a part of the problem, not a part of the solution.

Our second temptation develops as we regard our church in a changing world. Probably the greatest threat we face as individuals is the fact that we live now in an era of radical change. Continual and rapid change is the normal and inevitable pattern. This is a terrible fact to face openly. It requires that whole chunks of our traditional thinking and believing be revised. It is like asking a farm boy to get used to riding an escalator all day long.

When all else is changing so rapidly, it is tempting for us to want to treat the church as a sanctuary, not God's sanctuary so much as *our sanctuary, the one unchanging spot where we can find shelter from the buffeting of a changing world.* This is understandable. But, if we want this church to be a vital and effective force in God's changing world, we cannot and must not shield the church from change. We must be willing to expose our church to the same barrage of candid self-criticism that we use everywhere else to determine what must be preserved and what must be discarded.

It may be natural perhaps to reach defensively to suggested changes, clinging tightly to the church's past patterns without even asking ourselves if they are still relevant today. But these ways of reacting keep the church looking at its past, not its present.

The present age is simply not the past age. Certainly there can be no reasonable expectation that God will pour out his spirit to flow neatly and only in channels devised in the past, channels to which we are now comfortably accustomed.

We have inherited this church from the past. We are descended from great men who found strength in this church. But we must also pass this church on to those who come after us. And we must ask ourselves: How will we pass on this inheritance? Will it be diminished or increased? Will we pass along a church which is faithfully tuned to God's world today? Or will it be only a nostalgic reminder of an earlier and simpler world? Do we want our grandsons to find strength, or only shelter, in this church? Do we want to be the grandfathers, or only the grandsons, of great men?

MR. OVERFELT:

In summary, the prime concern of our church is local; that is, to meet the needs of its members through inspirational church services, opportunities to members to serve on boards, committees, et cetera, and through a good program of Christian education for our youngsters.

To be sure, our church should be interested in the outside world; but its ability to take effective action other than in our local area is severely limited, not only because of practical considerations, but also because of the lack of financial resources. There is little likelihood that our financial position can be bettered to permit us to do more than we are doing in the national and international fields.

As for each of us as good individual Christians, we must support our church to the best of our ability and participate actively

21

in its affairs. We must be good Samaritans in our everyday contacts with family, friends, associates, and strangers. We should keep interested in national and international affairs and participate actively and financially in those situations of greatest interest.

In the words of the early covenant of the First Church of Boston, which Mr. Post included in his message "One Point of Return" in our church bulletin of September 29, 1966, we "solemnly and religiously promise and bind ourselves to walk in all our ways according to the rule of the gospel, and in all sincere conformity to God's holy ordinances, and in mutual love and respect for one another, so as God shall give us grace."

A fierce restlessness grips the church today. The dialogue you have just read reveals something of this pervasive disquiet. The church is in crisis. This crisis is a dangerous opportunity in which God confronts us and calls us. We may use the crisis as an opportunity to move forward, or we may shrink back from fulfilling our function. How we respond will be conditioned by how we see ourselves and what process we engage in. This book is pointing to a pilgrim theology and a pilgrim's process. Not intending here to treat any issue exhaustively, I write in an indicative mood in hopes that you will be encouraged to use such a process to help your own local church face the crisis in which we are all so deeply immersed.

The process to which I point within the pilgrim style is: awareness of identity, situation definition, delineation of problems and imaginative projection of solutions, facing change and conflict, the planning process, training, and acting within the sphere of hope.

Chapter 1

The Pilgrim People
of God

Whenever a crisis engulfs us, a first step in our facing it is the discernment of identity: who are we? A man came to Karl Barth with the question, "What is the Bible?" The great theologian replied, "And who are you who ask?" When we raise the question of the crisis of the church today, its nature and meaning, the same question comes to us, "Who are you who ask?" Who we understand ourselves to be determines much of what we see and what our response will be.

This chapter is my response to the question of who we are as members of the local church. Here I try to describe our identity. I believe that no local church can face the present crisis creatively unless it first faces this question. When I try to describe our identity, the image that is most vivid for me is the "pilgrim people of God." The stance I think most appropriate for the church in the present crisis is the pilgrim stance.

WHO ARE THE PILGRIM PEOPLE OF GOD?

Anyone who becomes deeply concerned with his identity eventually finds himself investigating his family tree. When we who make up the membership of the local church today trace our spiritual ancestry, we go back through the centuries to a man by the name of Abraham. And we find a book that carries in it the early beginnings of our family history. Two passages from this book will serve as a kind of text to describe our identity:

> Now the Lord said to Abram, "Go from your country and your kindred and your father's house to the land that I will show you. And I will make of you a great nation, and I will bless you, and make your name great, so that you will be a blessing" (Gen. 12:1-2).

> By faith Abraham obeyed when he was called to go out to a place which he was to receive as an inheritance; and he went out, not knowing where he was to go. By faith he sojourned in the land of promise, as in a foreign land, living in tents with Isaac and Jacob, heirs with him of the same promise. For he looked forward to the city which has foundations, whose builder and maker is God (Heb. 11: 8-10).

Here we have the familiar beginning. A man confronted by God is called by him and enters into covenant with him. He sees a vision and is possessed by it. He goes on a journey into the unknown; he risks leaving the familiar, travels lightly, living in tents; he lives, responds, acts in order to be a blessing to others. He looks forward "to the city which has foundations, whose builder and maker is God."

From that point the story unfolds from a pilgrim man to a pilgrim people, down through the ages to right here and now, to you and me. The story proceeds from Abraham leaving Haran to Moses leaving Egypt, leading the children of Israel out of slavery, the long trek from Egypt led by a cloud by day and a pillar of fire by night. The wilderness wanderings show over and over again the pilgrim people's ambivalence about trusting the Lord who goes before them versus trusting in institutions such as kings and temples. Thus both literally and figuratively they wander in the wilderness. We follow them through the many stories of the kings and prophets in which over and over again the motif emerges: trust in the Lord who leads them into the future versus trust in "idols" which they can see and touch and taste and smell.

Colin Williams, in *Faith in a Secular Age,* points to the tension between the two motifs that the Roman Catholic scholar Leenhardt discovers in the Old Testament.

1. *The Abrahamic motif.* Israel is to be free to move away, like Abraham, . . . from all past securities, systems, laws, so as to be free to move out where God leads into uncharted territory.
2. *The Mosaic motif.* Israel must also be ready for her life to be given a definite shape so that the nations will be able to recognize the way of God. For this reason Israel is given its laws, its creed, its institutions.[1]

So we trace the history of the children of Israel, the pilgrim people of God, in every way an ordinary people, except for one great fact—their life is lived within the sphere of faith in the living God, who enters into covenant with them and calls them to live for the sake of the world. The history of the pilgrim people of God reaches a mighty crescendo in the coming of Jesus Christ, incarnation of the God who calls, covenants, and leads. As the Way which Abraham glimpsed from afar, Jesus is the very incarnation of pilgrimage.

The early church was a pilgrim church whose members spoke of their newfound faith as "the Way" (Acts 9:2; 19:9, 23; 22:4; 24:14). And, as the pilgrimage motif was dominant at the beginning, so we may see the whole history of the church, a history of a people and their God, a history of wilderness wandering and of forward movement and of promised land. For three centuries the early Christians were a minority group, often hunted, often suffering and dying because of their faith. The word witness means also "martyr"; for them witnessing and suffering were inseparable.

Things changed. Emperor Constantine accepted the church and gave it the task of Christianizing the whole civilization. Christians moved then from being a hunted group of pilgrims in a hostile world to a position of status and power. Later, with the rise of feudalism, the settled village system developed and with it the parish system—the village church, parallel to the area church in cities. For the last thousand years this type of church has been the primary institution for gathering Christians. The system made sense because life—residential, economic, social, and political—was centered in parishes, each with its own church.

But during the last one hundred and fifty years a change has been going on in the world, and it is now beginning to affect deeply the life of the church. The change was almost imperceptible at first, but now it is swirling around us, engulfing us. Undreamed of changes in science and technology are transforming our world. Almost certainly the church is in for as great changes as it experienced in the times of Constantine and of Martin Luther.

All through the centuries important models of the Christian pilgrimage have existed. During recent centuries the most prominent model among English-speaking Protestants has been that of Christian in John Bunyan's *Pilgrim's Progress*. Written in prison, this book describes the journey of Christian, a man who meets Evangelist and is set by him on the way to the heavenly Jerusalem. Leaving his earthly city, "the City of Destruction," Christian sets forth upon a lonely and adventuresome pilgrimage. A typical episode relates: "So I saw in my dream that the man began to run. Now he had not run so far from his own door, but his wife and children perceiving it, began to cry after him to return; but the man put his fingers in his ears, and ran on, crying, 'Life! Life! eternal life!' So he looked not behind him, but fled toward the middle of the plain." This model emphasized the individual, solitary aspect of pilgrimage, the uniqueness of each person in his relationship to the eternal. It emphasized a forsaking of this world, this Jerusalem, in favor of the heavenly Jerusalem.

Now a new model of Christian pilgrimage stands before the church—Dietrich Bonhoeffer. This model is strikingly different from the one in Bunyan's adventure in that, far from forsaking the affairs of this world, it preaches a deep commitment to the here and now. Out of obedience to God *this* Christian was involved deeply as a member of the German resistance movement and was in a plot to assassinate Hitler. Shortly before the end of World War II he was marched from his cell, stripped naked, and hanged until dead. His writings have had a powerful effect upon the life of the church and have strongly influenced the contemporary theology of mission. Shortly after his arrest, Bonhoeffer wrote these words from prison:

> During the last year or so I have come to appreciate the "worldliness" of Christianity as never before. The Christian is not a *homo religiosus,* but a man, pure and simple, just as Jesus was a man, compared with John the Baptist anyhow. I don't mean the shallow this-worldliness of the enlightened, of the busy, the comfortable or the lascivious. It's something much more profound than that, something in which the knowledge of death and resurrection is ever present. I believe Luther lived a this-worldly life in this sense. . . . It is only by living completely in this world that one learns to believe. One must abandon every attempt to

27

make something of oneself, whether it be a saint, a converted sinner, a churchman (the priestly type, so-called!), a righteous man or an unrighteous one, a sick man or a healthy one. This is what I mean by worldliness—taking life in one's stride, with all its duties and problems, its successes and failures, its experiences and helplessness. It is in such a life that we throw ourselves utterly into the arms of God and participate in his sufferings in the world and watch with Christ in Gethsemane. That is faith, that is *metanoia,* and that is what makes a man and a Christian (cf. Jeremiah 45). How can success make us arrogant or failure lead us astray, when we participate in the sufferings of God by living in this world? [2]

There is no doubt that Bonhoeffer has captured the imagination and challenged the spirits of many people in our churches. This contemporary model rather than Bunyan's Christian will dominate our thinking about pilgrimage in this generation. But we must not give up entirely the Bunyan model. These models highlight different aspects of Christian pilgrimage; we must not think of them as entirely separate. Bonhoeffer would rejoice in Christian's steadfastness as he risks all to reach the heavenly city, although he would deny that that pilgrimage can go on any longer without a full absorption in this world.

We who are the pilgrim people of God in this time stand at the threshold of a new age. We have a decision to make. A new country opens before us. Will our response be one of joy and faithfulness or one of fear and wilderness wandering? Are we willing to move out where God leads into uncharted territory? These are the pilgrim questions that will be before us in this book.

CHARACTERISTICS OF THE PILGRIM STYLE

Abraham, with whom we began, will suffice to introduce the crucial characteristics of pilgrimage.

1. *Encounter with God.* "Now the Lord said to Abram, 'Go.' " To Abraham, God was real, personally confronting

him with a call. So it has been with all pilgrim spirits through the ages. The confrontation and call have come in multitudinous ways. They have come as an experiencing of the wholly other, as the transcendent, as the Christ in the midst, as the Christ in "the least of these my brethren." In this book God is spoken of and pointed to essentially as the one who discloses himself in the biblical witness, the God of history who summons us.

2. *Vision.* "Where there is no vision the people perish." Where there is no vision the person perishes. Abraham saw it, though dimly, when "by faith" he "obeyed when he was called to go out to a place which he was to receive as an inheritance." Vision is a futuristic word; it hooks up not only into the now but even more into the future. A man who has seen a vision is willing to undergo untold hardships; he is willing to work, to sacrifice, to give life itself in order that the future may be born. Without vision life tends to be a meaningless grind; man is a plodder, given to seeing only in the moment, if there, the meaning of existence. The feel of vision is joy and hope. To the man of vision life is pilgrimage, a state of mind before it is a journey; for him tomorrow is always the frontier, the unexplored country.

3. *Openness to the future.* Abraham did not see his vision with clarity: "He went out, not knowing where he was to go. By faith he sojourned in the land of promise, as in a foreign land." The risk of openness emerges in the light of the encounter with God and in the light of vision. Without risking openness one never leaves the Harans; one lives safely on plateaus, seeking always to secure whatever gains one has, dull, listless, flat, and fat. All the forward progress made by man and nations has been on the basis of this kind of risk.

4. *Living in tents.* This aspect of pilgrimage highlights the fact that on earth we have no abiding place and that our

ultimate trust is to be in God only. In some deep sense we are just passing through. Here we have also the insight that pilgrimage is dynamic rather than static. Pilgrimage is not on the side of putting ultimate trust in any institutional forms, codes, or systems. Intellectually as well as spiritually we are to be mobile. To live "in tents" is to be ever on the way in our thinking, always questioning, not expecting final answers. To live in tents means that the pilgrim can never rest uncritically with the status quo, for he is lured by a vision and goaded by a divine discontent.

5. *Living for others.* "Go from your country and your kindred and your father's house to the land that I will show you . . . so that you will be a blessing." Here we have the height of pilgrimage—to live for others, to be pro-existent. Abraham, the children of Israel, and all of this spirit who come after bear this mark and this call, to be like Jesus Christ, the man for others.

6. *Faith and hope.* "By faith Abraham obeyed when he was called. . . . He looked forward to the city which has foundations, whose builder and maker is God." He goes believing the God who called him, and his very going is hope in action. All great pilgrims who have blessed us in the past, and all great pilgrims who bless us in our time, have possessed this great gift of believing that we do not act alone but that he who calls us also prepares the way before us.

WHAT KIND OF GOD DO WE BELIEVE IN?

The pilgrim people find their identity in their relationship to God, and they act out their faith as they understand his nature and his will. In each age pilgrims have to find ways of speaking of their God intelligibly. Our family history is written in the Old and New Testaments, in church history, and in the creeds and platforms of the churches. But each pilgrim person must experience the meaning of that faith, and each generation must appropriate it afresh and learn to speak of it in terms that make sense to contemporaries. So, how shall we speak about God today? Here are some guidelines.

We believe in the God of creation. The book that contains the beginning of our family history begins with these words: "In the beginning God created the heavens and the earth." God is thus not identical with his creation. For primitive man, everything is alive, divine, and may be worshiped. Not so with us; only God is to be worshiped, not his creation (his creatures). The book continues: "God created man in his own image. . . . The Lord God formed man of dust from the ground, and breathed into his nostrils the breath of life; and man became a living being." God gives man dominion over the earth, over the fish of the sea, over the fowl of the air, and over every living thing that moves upon the earth. Man has dominion and is responsible to God for his stewardship.

We believe in the God who loves the world. I remember distinctly a picture in one of the books in my clergyman father's study, an etching of an ark caught in a terrible storm. On the ark were the church members, and they were looking at (some were reaching out to) many people caught in the turbulent seas. The teaching was apparent. In the ark (the church) was salvation; outside, destruction. By implication, the great imperative for the Christian is to get as many people into the ship as possible.

The doctrine of salvation in the Bible carries two important themes. In the Old Testament it has a clear this-worldly significance—peace, joy, forgiveness, justice, security, prosperity, and the beginnings of the concept of deliverance from death. While this significance is present

31

in the teachings of Christ and the apostles, the concept of salvation as being deliverance in the final judgment is definitely there also. But the background teaching of both Testaments is that God intends the salvation of the whole world. There is a growing consensus among biblical scholars that it is the salvation of the world which God intends and that it is the task of the church to show forth the meaning of the reign of God and to indicate to the whole world its Lord.

We gain some insight into this aspect of our belief when we remember that history is the arena of God's action. When we think about history we are likely to think in terms of the past, something that has already happened. But history is a process, something going on, and God is involved in the process of history. The church is a part of the process of world history, the world that God loves. It was into world history that Christ was born; incarnation, crucifixion, and resurrection are part of world history. Thus, when we speak of God's acting now, we speak of a God who operates in the here and now of history, *our* history. Jesus was fully committed to this world, living in it as the man for others. It is the faith of the Christian pilgrim that the resurrected Lord's presence—the Holy Spirit—is transforming the world in which we live and directing it toward its intended and promised end.

We believe in the God who hates bondage. God created man and gave him dominion over the creation. But all is not well with man. The Genesis story reveals that God's purpose for man has not been realized. Man falls short of it by turning away from God, and the results of that turning are alienation from God; alienation from himself; alienation from his brother; and alienation from true community.

He has become subject to the principalities and powers over which he was given dominion.

But God does not leave man alone. He comes to him. He hates the bondage in which man is held, and carries out his mission to free him. This is the story of salvation in the Scriptures. It is beautifully set forth in the story of the exodus, and reaches its climax in the resurrection of Jesus Christ. In Jesus Christ we see a life in which the alienations are overcome. In him we have the fulfillment and the promise of the new creation.

Hans Hoekendijk has written meaningfully about the goal of God's mission as the establishment of *shalom*. In *The Church Inside Out,* he writes:

> Shalom is much more than personal salvation. It is at once peace, integrity, community, harmony, and justice. Its rich content can be felt in Psalm 85 where we read that shalom is . . . where "mercy and truth are met together; righteousness and peace have kissed each other. Truth shall spring out of the earth; and righteousness shall look down from heaven."
>
> The Messiah is the prince of shalom (Isaiah 9:6), he shall be the shalom (Micah 5:5), he shall speak shalom unto the heathen (Zechariah 9:10); or, in the prophecy of Jeremiah (29:11), he will realize the plans of shalom, which the Lord has in mind for us, to give us a future and hope.
>
> In the New Testament, God's shalom is the most elementary expression of what life in the new aeon actually is. Jesus leaves shalom with his disciples— "Shalom I leave with you; my shalom I give unto you" (John 14:27), and the preaching of the apostles is summarized as "preaching shalom through Jesus Christ" (Acts 10:36; cf. Isaiah 52:7). "We are ambassadors therefore on behalf of Christ, . . . working together with him" to proclaim "now is the day of shalom" (2 Cor. 5:20; 6:1-2).[3]

We may discern that the great awakening text for the local church in our time is the one associated with the time

33

when Jesus rose in the synagogue to read from the book of the prophet Isaiah:

" The Spirit of the Lord is upon me,
    because he has anointed me to preach good news to the poor.
    He has sent me to proclaim release to the captives
    and recovering of sight to the blind,
    to set at liberty those who are oppressed,
    to proclaim the acceptable year of the Lord."

And he closed the book, and gave it back to the attendant, and sat down; and the eyes of all in the synagogue were fixed on him. And he began to say to them, "Today this scripture has been fulfilled in your hearing" (Luke 4:18-21).

We believe in the God who covenants with us. The same God who covenanted with Abraham covenants with us. He covenants with us as he covenanted with Moses, calling him to participate with him in setting the captives free. We live under his promise "I will be with you." This same God covenants with us in baptism, the Lord's Supper, confirmation, marriage, and ordination. He is the same God of the covenant of Sinai who says, "You shall have no other gods before me" (Exod. 20:3), therefore forbidding the absolutizing of any institutions or human values.

We believe in the God of the wilderness wandering. God saved the children of Israel from bondage in Egypt. But because of their disobedience they wandered in the wilderness for forty years before reaching the promised land. A generation died murmuring against God and Moses and the new commandments. Jesus was in the wilderness forty days after his baptism. The concept of wilderness is an important pilgrimage concept.

As Christian pilgrims we believe that God does not forsake us either in the wilderness of moral waste or in the wilderness of testing or punishment, that he continues to covenant with us in the wilderness, and that the wilderness itself may be the very beginning of renewal.

In a sense the local church is in the wilderness today. Whether we are there because of unfaithfulness or because we are being punished or tested, we may have the assurance that we are not alone. He who led the children of Israel by a cloud by day and a pillar of fire by night is with us and goes before us. He is at work in the world. Some of our prophets today are saying that the way out of the wilderness is to join him in his work in the world.

Chapter 2

The Watershed Issue

THE CHURCH EXISTS in the midst of the world and must minister in this world of here and now, not in an age that is past. It must shape its life around the right now with its eyes fixed on a world being born. In this chapter I propose to take a look at the world around us, the situation in which the church is set. A text might be "Behold, I make all things new" (Rev. 21:5)—for newness, change, and revolution characterize our age. As Robert Oppenheimer summarized it:

> This world of ours is a new world in which the unity of knowledge, the nature of human communities, the order of society, the order of ideas, the very notions of society and culture have changed and will not return to what they have been in the past. . . . One thing that is new is the prevalence of newness, the changing scope and scale of change itself, so that the world alters as we walk in it, so that the years of man's life measure not some small growth or rearrangement or moderation of what he learned in childhood, but a great upheaval.[1]

Some of the newness and change has been with us for a long time, but we just haven't been aware of it. Some has been long in coming and was foreseen. Some has come upon us with the surprise and shock of an earthquake.

In trying to help us discern our present situation, Walter W. Sikes interprets Paul Valery, an eminent French essayist, philosopher, and social scientist, who

distinguishes between "epochs" as referring to those long stretches of history which maintain a certain identity of character and stability, within which change goes on slowly and without crisis, and "periods" as referring to those moments in history which mark the beginning and the end respectively of epochs, when like a landslide or an avalanche the forces which are long in formation suddenly are set in motion, perhaps by some apparently minor and obscure event, to alter quickly, radically, and irreversibly the whole scene.[2]

Historians have little difficulty pointing to the periods when one epoch ended and another began. When the Christian idea exploded in the world, the cultures of the Greco-Roman world were radically altered. During the fourth and fifth centuries, the ancient world came to an end and a new one that was to last almost a millennium was born. Then the medieval world disintegrated and Western man entered the Renaissance. Something culture-shaking entered history with the industrial revolution. Within our own lifetime, an old age died and a new one was born with the dropping of the atom bombs on Hiroshima and Nagasaki.

Science and technology are the parents of this new age. Physicist Harold Schilling says, "Science is the great transformer. Not since the emergence of Christianity itself has there appeared a more potent transformer of the world and of life than science." [3] Many local church members do not agree that the age is new. They say there always has been change and always will be and that it only *seems* that current changes are more radical than those our fathers lived through. They suspect that this talk about change is just a trick to keep things stirred up. Well, let's take a closer look. My contention is that science and technology have drastically changed the ways in which man produces goods, the manner in which he lives, and his very ways of perceiving the world, himself, and the future. Inherent in these changes are great hopes and dangers; and the church, if it is going to minister faithfully in this age, must be duly cognizant of these hopes and dangers.

THE CYBERNETIC AGE

The electronic computer is the symbol of the new age. Its vacuum-tube form appeared in 1946. Shortly thereafter the invention of the transistor greatly reduced the computer's size and has greatly increased its availability, founding the present $6.4 billion computer industry. There is little doubt that it, along with the industries and discoveries related to it, are transforming the age in which we live, giving birth to the cybernetic[4] age.

Donald N. Michael, resident fellow of the Institute for Policy Studies, Washington, D.C., described the participant character of these servomechanisms.

Cybernated systems perform with a precision and a rapidity unmatched in humans. They also perform in ways that would be impractical or impossible for humans to duplicate. They can be built to detect and correct errors in their own performance and to indicate to men which of their components are producing the error. They can make judgments on the basis of instructions programmed into them. They can remember and search their memories for appropriate data, which either have been programmed into them along with their instructions or have been acquired in the process of manipulating new data. Thus, they can learn on the basis of past experience with their environment. They can receive information in more codes and sensory modes than men can.

They are beginning to perceive and recognize. . . . Cybernation presages changes in the social system so vast and so different from those with which we have traditionally wrestled that it will challenge to their roots our current perceptions about the viability of our way of life.[5]

At first it was thought that the computer was just one more handy gadget in the industrial age. In 1950 there were fifteen in use; in 1966 there were 40,000; and it is expected that in 1970 there will be 70,000. William D. Smith has said, "If computers were suddenly withdrawn from service both government and business operations would come almost to a standstill." [6]

One of the breathtaking attributes of the computer is its ability to work at incredible speed. "This speed is such that a modern computer can perform more calculations in one hour than a football stadium full of scientists could do in a lifetime." [7] A layman can get some glimpse of its capacities by looking at a January, 1967, *Fortune* advertisement of a computer that can "control a manufacturing process, run a payroll, analyze a missile firing problem, update an inventory, and carry on separate conversations with over two hundred individuals at remote consoles. All at the same time."

American business is preparing for the radical impact of the computer on our society:

The American Telephone and Telegraph Company expects in the future that half of their circuits will be used by persons giving or receiving information to or from computers or by computers doing the same with other computers. Computers will communicate globally at nanosecond speed (a nanosecond is to a second what a second is to thirty years), yet at the same time individuals by using portable equipment will be able to secure information, send and receive personal messages, and do their bookkeeping while playing golf.[8]

In time scarcely an aspect of life will remain untouched and unchanged by the cybernetic revolution, whether it be the way children will be educated, medicine will be practiced, vast institutions will be administered, law will be practiced, or police work will be carried out.

Three computer-related characteristics of this new age need to be considered. Each bears the marks of newness and carries both great threat and great promise.

1. *Man possesses the means of production whereby all the people of the world may be fed, housed, and tooled.* Because of the linking of the computer with beltline machinery, there is in principle no effective limit to our productive abilities. U Thant, secretary-general of the United Nations, has expressed this myth-shattering fact in the following words:

> The truth, the central stupendous truth, about developed countries today is that they can have in anything but the shortest run the kind and scale of resources they decide to have. . . . It is no longer resources that limit decisions. It is the decision that makes the resources. This is the fundamental revolutionary change, perhaps the most revolutionary mankind has ever known.[9]

But, for man to be able to fulfill the dream "that all have enough and to spare" we must solve the problem of distribution; and that solution appears to be far off.

2. *Mankind possesses the power to commit suicide.* There is no longer any doubt that man has the capability to destroy his life, if indeed not all life on this planet. Here Robert Theobold states:

> The fact that there are now sufficient nuclear explosives available to destroy civilization if not all of life, is now regarded almost as a cliché. New depth and meaning were, however, recently given to this realization in an article published in the *Scientific American* by Herbert York and Jerome Wiesner, both of whom have held high office in recent Administrations. They stated: "The clearly

predictable course of the arms race is a steady downward spiral into oblivion." The existence of the drive toward unlimited destructive power therefore condemns each country to undermine its own security in the very process of pursuing it.[10]

Alongside population control, war control is man's other most urgent task. For both, all that is lacking is the dedicated will—man already has the knowledge, skills, basic technology, and processes.

3. *The computer will force man's mind out of the repetitive productive system, creating job crises and opening new possibilities for leisure.* There is no repetitive task which the computer cannot do better than a human being. As the computer becomes more and more sophisticated, it will take over all tasks where the decision-making rules can be set out in advance. Gerard Piel, publisher of the *Scientific American,* says:

> The new development in our technology is the replacement of the human nervous system by automatic control units at each point in the production process. The human muscle began to be disengaged from the productive process at least a hundred years ago. Now the human nervous system is being disengaged.[11]

There is no consensus as to how cybernation will affect jobs. Some think Americans are headed for serious unemployment; others believe that as fast as jobs disappear new kinds of jobs will be born because of the new technologies. But there is no doubt that the jobs which will be created will require workers with higher skills. The sign in the New York subways—"You can't get tomorrow's job with yesterday's skills"—is a portent of things to come. Walter W. Sikes points up the problem:

> This process, which is creating vast new economic goals and possibilities, is also creating increasingly great pools of unemployment,

41

and not only among the more unskilled but among the more high-skilled and professional workers. Whether this unemployment is transitory or permanent depends on decisions yet to be made. In America somewhere between 40,000 and 70,000 jobs are disappearing each week (the estimates vary depending on the criteria used) while half that many new workers are being sent into the labor market by the population explosion. Between 1964 and 1974 more than 15,000,000 jobs will be wiped out by cybernation and some 26,000,000 additional workers will be added to the American blue-collar and white-collar labor force. This would seem to mean that we must create 4,000,000 new jobs per year or find radically new ways of distributing our income and using our time.[12]

The cybernetic revolution can no more be stopped than could its predecessor, the industrial revolution. (And some are calling cybernetics "the second industrial revolution.") As time passes, mankind will be delivered from dull work which engages his time and attention in repetitive motions which machines can do better; in such tasks man is an underefficient and overexpensive worker. Thus, man will be freed to do more creative work. What this means in terms of new leisure and what this means economically is now being hotly debated, for it raises problems in almost every field—education and culture, economics and politics, philosophy and religion.

THE POPULATION EXPLOSION

Ravaged constantly by predators and plagues, the earth's human population grew slowly. It took a million or more years for the population to reach a billion. This happened somewhere around 1800. But the second billion was added in little over a century, and every indication is that by the year 2000 there will be over six billion of us!

This population explosion is man's most severe problem. Modern science and technology have overcome many ancient enemies of mankind; diseases that used to destroy

42

whole populations have been conquered; babies who formerly would have died live to have more babies. We apparently are heading for a massive food crisis unless warnings are heeded and birth control enforced.

BIOLOGICAL ENGINEERING

Scarcely any field of human endeavor has made such striking advances as biochemistry, paving the way for biological engineering to an extent scarcely imagined only a few years ago. Donald Michael says:

> In future years we will see biological engineering being used to alter the genetic code which transfers to the next generation the direction for its nature and form. There will also be an increasing capacity to manipulate the organism once it is born, to increase the size of the brain or the heart or other organs by the selective use of chemicals before and after birth, to transplant organs from human to human and to replace human organs with electromechanical substitutes. And we shall also see biological engineering used to modify emotional states and mental abilities. Telemetering and computer techniques already in use for monitoring, diagnosing, and treating biological malfunctions will be greatly refined and extended.[13]

Lynton K. Caldwell, in the *Yale Review,* describes the relationship of biological engineering and the population explosion:

> The coincident and related explosions of human population and of biological knowledge may conceivably represent the most critical stage in human evolution since the last great ice age. The ability and necessity to control the numbers and hence (in some respects) the genetic characteristics of future populations could create a situation without precedent in human existence. And, in addition, the availability and refinement of chemopsychiatric drugs suggests both hoped for and frightening possibilities for the manipulation and control of human behavior. Never before have the

necessity and the possibility of control over man occurred at so decisive a conjunction.[14]

URBANIZATION

As a result of these various revolutions, there has been a worldwide mass movement into urban centers. A World Health Organization study made in 1964 concluded that only 10 percent of the world's population will be working in agriculture by A.D. 2000. By that year the probabilities are that the world's population will be doubled and that the additional three billion human beings will be living in urban areas.[15] In this country alone the urban population more than doubled in 1910-60, increasing from almost 42 million to 112.5 million. Two thirds of our people now live in large metropolitan areas. By 1980 the population over age 65 will have increased by almost 30 percent; and by that time approximately 80 percent of those in the United States will be living in urban areas. Cities that are now separate will be merging into megalopolises stretching from Norfolk to Bangor, from Minneapolis to St. Louis, from San Francisco to San Diego.

The urban center has become the center of power, of culture, and of the massive problems of our time. Inner-city public education is usually of inferior quality, with overcrowded schools and severe racial and ethnic tensions. Employment problems need constant attention—the training and retraining of workers, the plight of the Negro as the last one hired and the first one fired, the in-migrants' agonies of adjustment. Housing problems are almost untouched. Public housing has stressed efficiency rather than human values, and urban renewal projects become new-style slums. Every metropolitan area faces the problems of poverty, the communities of the left-behind, too many

44

people, high rates of illegitimacy and broken marriages, poor mass transportation, and changing values.

The metropolis of one million to ten million has become the dominant political unit of our time. It is a paradox, throbbing with life and power and fraught with massive human problems.

SECULARIZATION

The fantastic advances in science and technology have already converted much of the earth into a new-style home for man. What is happening to his image of himself, his view of his world, and his values as he lives in this new home? Man's image of himself is changing, his view of his world is changing, and his values are changing. Certain areas of life used to be considered unquestionable, inviolable. Now everything is questioned and accounted for in terms of human disposition and scientific analysis. Man considers himself autonomous (self-governing) without need of transcendent laws. He thinks he can derive his standards and goals from his own reason and from the natural and social environments. This world has become the focus of his attention.

Harvey Cox, who has given secularization a positive theological interpretation, defines it as follows:

[Secularization] is the loosing of the world from religious and quasi-religious understandings of itself, the dispelling of all closed world views, the breaking of all supernatural myths and sacred symbols. It represents what another observer has called the "defatalization of history," the discovery by man that he has been left with the world on his hands, and that he can no longer blame fortune or the furies for what he does with it. Secularization is man turning his attention away from worlds beyond and toward this world and this time (*saeculum*—"this present age"). It is what Dietrich Bonhoeffer in 1944 called "man's coming of age." [16]

45

The secular style has been long in process; few doubt that it is the style of contemporary man.

THE EMERGENCE OF GLOBAL MAN

Thanks to technology, particularly as it affects communication and travel, the world has shrunk into a rather small planet. Time and space have been virtually eliminated. More and more the nations of the world are seeing themselves as interdependent. It is now possible to have instantaneous communication all over the globe. What is done in one nation immediately reverberates in all the others. Although there was a time when autonomous communities had a rationale for separateness, that time is no more. The words of John Donne become increasingly clear: "No man is an island." Indeed, in our time no nation or even a group of nations is an island; we are bound together in a single bundle of mankind. We have moved into the era of global history.

THE REVOLUTION IN RISING EXPECTATIONS

Most of the people in the world are poor, with more living below the subsistence level than ever before in history. The gap between the haves and the have-nots is constantly widening. When these awesome facts are put together with the increased education of the leaders of poor nations, the communication and travel revolutions, and the economic progress of the industrialized Western world, the background for what has been aptly called the revolution in rising expectations becomes apparent.

In the last few decades there has been a massive reaction against imperialism and colonialism. Since 1943, fifty-four independent nations have come into being out of the fragments of old empires and have taken their places in the United Nations. Their independence has come, in many

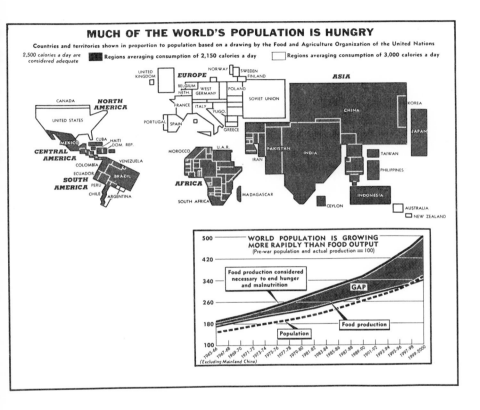

MUCH OF THE WORLD'S POPULATION IS HUNGRY

Countries and territories shown in proportion to population based on a drawing by the Food and Agriculture Organization of the United Nations

2,500 calories a day are considered adequate ◼ Regions averaging consumption of 2,150 calories a day ☐ Regions averaging consumption of 3,000 calories a day

EUROPE
UNITED KINGDOM
NORWAY SWEDEN FINLAND
BELGIUM NETH. WEST GERMANY POLAND
FRANCE ITALY YUGO.
PORTUGAL SPAIN
GREECE
SOVIET UNION

ASIA
CHINA
KOREA
JAPAN
TAIWAN
PHILIPPINES
INDONESIA

NORTH AMERICA
CANADA
UNITED STATES

CENTRAL AMERICA
MEXICO CUBA HAITI DOM. REP.

SOUTH AMERICA
COLOMBIA VENEZUELA
ECUADOR BRAZIL
PERU
CHILE ARGENTINA

AFRICA
MOROCCO U.A.R.
IRAN PAKISTAN INDIA
SOUTH AFRICA MADAGASCAR CEYLON

AUSTRALIA
NEW ZEALAND

WORLD POPULATION IS GROWING MORE RAPIDLY THAN FOOD OUTPUT
(Pre-war population and actual production = 100)

500
420
340
260
180
100

Food production considered necessary to end hunger and malnutrition

GAP

Food production

Population

1965-66 1967-68 1969-70 1971-72 1973-74 1975-76 1977-78 1979-80 1981-82 1983-84 1985-86 1987-88 1989-90 1991-92 1993-94 1995-96 1997-98 1999-2000

(Excluding Mainland China)

instances after long-suffering, as a dream fulfilled. These countries face the awesome task of nation-building, and most are without the necessary trained leaders or adequate capital. Their inability to compete in world markets causes no little resentment. No large nation has clean hands. All have been engaged in exploitative practices, control of raw materials, manipulation of raw material prices, class and caste discrimination. The hungry and the deprived have strong feelings of resentment against the well-fed and powerful.

In the United States the revolution in rising expectations has taken the forms of the civil rights movement and the war on poverty. The goals of human dignity, better education, better housing, better health, and economic democracy are not so different from those which the new African demands; important changes have come about, but there is a mounting frustration among the Negro young people and the poor. The revolution has not ended. Change is slow, tragically slow.

Chapter 3

Ethics and Belief

THANKS TO COMPUTER-RELATED scientific and technological advances, in the midst of the greatest knowledge
explosion ever known, two million scientific experiments
are reported annually. Knowledge in virtually every field
is doubling every decade.[1] Since 1957, the year the Rus-
sians lofted Sputnik, the United States government has
tripled its support of research and development; the 1966
budget allotted fifteen billion dollars for this purpose. And
the knowledge explosion is only well begun.

Knowledge is dynamic. Men possess it and men use it to
transform human existence and environment. As knowledge
grows, the world changes and so does human behavior.
This response affects the way people make decisions and
the way people believe, two crisis areas in the new age.

THE ETHICAL CRISIS

The world has grown so small in time and distance and
so large because of the new knowledge that ethical matters
have become amazingly complex and increasingly am-

biguous. The grandfather in us longs for another day when things seemed simple and undebatable.

Under the heading "The Cybernetic Age" I mentioned three new promises and threats. First, there is unlimited productive power. Even the blindest man can see that something is tragically wrong with a world in which unlimited production is possible, yet millions starve. Whose task is it to think about the complex problems of the distribution of the world's goods in a world where time and space have practically been obliterated? When some of us were children, "India's coral strand" was far, far away, and tales of leprosy and starvation even had a slightly romantic touch; now the starving are in our backyard. Who prepares the ground for a people to think in new ways and act in new ways now that new possibilities are with us? What new political and economic structures are needed now that God has opened the gates to an era in which man's old enemy, hunger, may be defeated?

Second, there is unlimited destructive power. The problems of war and peace loom large in any age. They loom especially large in a time when the weapons of war have grown so vast that they stagger the imagination. Who is to create the climate in which we can grapple with man's long record of killing and maiming? How can we reconcile the religion of nationalism with the emergence of a world long waiting to be born, when "nation shall not lift up sword against nation, neither shall they learn war any more"? Surely the justification of war itself in this new time has become ambiguous—even of the so-called just war. Yet we war, and men and women and children, military and civilians, suffer and die. Any war is an ethical crisis. It always has been. But now, with unlimited destruction in our power, it is especially so. The Rev. Harriet B. Kurtz, a specialist in this field, asks, "How can technology and moral concern collaborate to engender political will and prepare the way for governmental action toward eventual development of global safety authority to control war around the world?" [2]

Third, there is freedom from repetitive production tasks. Throughout the centuries we have understood life in terms of work, receiving much of our identity from the work we do. Now cybernated production threatens to free men from certain dull tasks which the machine can do better. But what can life mean without work? Particularly, what will it mean for many who simply are not qualified to fulfill complex creative assignments whether or not remunerated? What are the ethics of not being needed? What are the ethical implications of the new leisure reluctantly faced by hundreds of thousands of people—by millions of people around history's corner? What is the new image of man emerging here?

The population explosion. The checks and balances that formerly kept the population within bounds are being removed by science. In the midst of a population explosion which even by conservative estimates threatens to engulf the world in a vast famine, what are the ethics of limiting this population? To what extent should social engineering become a factor? Should limits be set on the number of children each family can have? Should the state permit only certain people to have them, or sterilize all women after, say, the third birth? Now that the genetic code can be altered, should governments determine what kind of children should be born—how many with high competence in engineering, soldiering, teaching?

Disparity between rich and poor. As for the growing disparity between the rich and the poor, how can we eat in

51

peace or rest in peace if we do not struggle for a world where hunger will be overcome for all? Advances made in the field of biochemistry open up wide and threatening ethical questions. Already scientists have passed an important barrier; they have created a living virus. Have they created "life," or is that step just around the corner? Persons are "adjusted" by the use of stimulants and tranquilizers which directly affect and regulate moods and feelings. More and more diseases are being conquered, and many of the new discoveries and advances will postpone death. Eventually a time may come when the government will have to determine when certain people will die to make room for others. Yet a recent newspaper report told the story of a California incurable whose body had been frozen at death, to be thawed out when medical science has conquered the disease and mastered the process of rejuvenation.

Highly sophisticated experimentation is going on with human embryonic material to gain important information about genetics and development so as to be able to reduce birth defects and disease. How long should the embryo be permitted to live? What is destroyed when life is ended? What should be done with the embryo when the experiment is over? With the invention of the pill and the ring many of the old inhibitors of premarital intercourse have been substantially weakened. Will it suffice for the church to stick with its old counsel, acting as though nothing has changed?

Urbanization. Urbanization means cities, big cities, big cities burgeoning and decaying. What kind of ethics can look on slums as necessary, water and air pollution as something we must accept? What kind of ethics permits the best leadership and the greatest amount of money to move out of the city, allowing the inner city to sink deeper and deeper into financial trouble, and giving rise to the rot of the inner city where communities of the left-behind earn their living in dull and ill-paid jobs? The city teems with people, people who suffer. Wherever suffering is, one or more ethical problems are signaled. How shall we act responsibly now that we are an urban culture?

Rising expectations. The revolution of rising expectations carries the ingrained evil of man's inhumanity to man and raises ethical problems of his housing and employment opportunities, and his need for self-respect regardless of his skin color or ethnic background. The problem of prejudice, which has been with us so long, has become acute because, like it or not, the world is now one and most of the people of the world are not WASPs (White, Anglo-Saxon, Protestants).

Do we need to expand our traditional moral codes? Many of us have long thought that the answer to ethical problems could be found simply by looking in "the Book." There have always been some who doubted this approach, but now the doubters among committed Christians have greatly increased in number. One, Harold K. Schilling, Christian and scientist, has written in the field of science and religion.[3] He thinks man has marched off the map. He states why old moral codes are held to be inadequate with respect to contemporary life:

First, they have been concerned largely with individual, personal morality, to the almost complete exclusion of group morality. Second, they entirely disregard large areas of life. One of these is man's relationship to nature, which problem area was not important morally until recently.

Let us look at the decalogue in the light of these remarks. The first four of its commandments pertain to relations between a person and God: You shall have no other gods beside me; you shall not make for yourself and worship an image of God; you shall not swear falsely by the name of the Lord; remember the Sabbath day and keep it holy to the Lord. The other six pertain to relationships between persons: honor your parents, do not murder, commit adultery, steal, bear false witness, or covet what belongs to your neighbor. Far be it from me to belittle these moral principles. They are still binding, though it must also be admitted that they need to be interpreted for each situation, and then applied responsibly, not blindly. I do suggest, however, that they offer little wisdom relative to the ethic of many of the most pressing problems of our day, especially those that involve more than individual person-to-person relationship, and call for moral decisions by groups.[4]

Dr. Schilling presents his list:

> nuclear, chemical, and biological warfare
> equal rights for minorities and majorities
> minimization or elimination of poverty
> consequences of the population explosion
> > probability of insufficient food
> > birth management
> > death management
> labor and automation
> > elimination of job types
> > retraining
> > relocation
> leisure management
> behavioral engineering, the transformation and
> > management of persons, of groups, or
> > entire peoples
> prenatal genetic control
> conservation of nature
> > disaster control
> > plant and animal
> > crop improvement
> growth of knowledge and the management
> > of its consequences.[5]

55

Dr. Schilling thinks that the scientific community, at last waking up to its ethical responsibility, should join hands with the religious community to face the new ethical problems all around us. What do *you* think? Does the scientific community belong in the field of ethics? Is this the province of religion alone? What are our religious communities doing to face these new crises?

Are we who believe in the God of creation who assigned man dominion immersed sufficiently in the question of what man is doing with this stewardship? We who are ourselves children of the exodus and believe in the God whose mission it is to set man free to be man, are we sufficiently involved now as untold millions make their exodus from misery and starvation and second-class citizenship? And we who worship the God of the covenant, who says, "You shall have no other gods before me," as we experience the relativization of values, are we willing to do the work necessary to find our way to clarity and right action?

THE BELIEF CRISIS

Chapter 2 defined the following components of secularization:

The loosing of the world from a religious and quasi-religious understanding of itself.

The dispelling of all closed world views, the breaking of all supernatural myths and sacred symbols.

The discovery by man that he has been left with the world on his hands and that he can no longer blame fortune or the furies for what he does with it.

The turning of attention away from worlds beyond and toward this world and this time.

Most of us in the local church will agree that the process described has been going on not only in relation to "modern man" in the abstract but in us as well. The extent to which it has gone on and the rapidity with which it has gone on measure the severity of the crisis in an individual or a group.

Erik H. Erikson, in *Childhood and Society*,[6] says that a crisis of identity takes place whenever a person enters a new stage of development. It occurs in infancy and through all the stages from infancy to adulthood. A crisis of belief occurs also for individuals and for groups whenever they enter any new stage of development. Since mankind has entered such a new stage now, it is not surprising that a belief crisis should be an aspect of the age in which we are living.

Man's new home is the metropolis, for thinking is now everywhere shaped by the urban centers.[7] Man is highly mobile, largely anonymous, pragmatic ("Will it work?"), and primarily concerned about this world, not the next. He lives a fragmented existence. He may reside with his family in one community, work in another, worship in another, and spend important leisure in another. Each community knows only a part of him, and he probably has no depth-knowledge of any community. No one knows him fully any-more, and so he has difficulty knowing himself as a unitary man.

The American is born into a culture with a knowledge explosion, an affluent society, a society that puts a high premium on having a good time. This world has opened up many new freedoms to him. He has the best food, good medical care. He does not look upon this life as a valley of tears, full of pain and woe, from which death will soon deliver him; rather he likes it here and wants to stay. As a matter of fact, he wants to stay as long as he can. Some-how the old message he has heard in church, or thinks he has heard, doesn't fit these new feelings and possibilities.

Of course many modern men still go to church. Questioned, they prove to know little about the Old or New Testaments and not much of church history; when it comes to doctrine, they tend to lump it all with the ten commandments (which they very likely cannot recite) and the golden rule. Will Herberg is well known for describing the paradoxical situation: Americans are becoming more religious and more secular.

Modern man feels a gap between the world of the church and the world of his real existence. But he has genuine feelings about the church—warm, sentimental feelings. He wants to protect the church because he feels that it is the container of important values in his way of life, but he is separating himself more and more from its message.

Yet we must recognize that there are also many in our society for whom belief in God is no longer a live option. They have left the church with "no hard feelings," but they are just as gone as they would be had they stormed out in a rage. They have resolved the crisis: God does not exist.

Many stay in the church for reasons that are not altogether clear to them. They remain with longing in their hearts; they no longer really believe, but they continue to hope that some word will be spoken which will catch fire in them and authenticate and fulfill their longing.

The death of God? Recently *Time* magazine startled the nation with a black-and-red cover that asked, "Is God Dead?" The feature article fascinatingly described the belief crisis and the theologians who are alternatively called radical, secular, or death-of-God. These theologians had been writing for some time, but the article brought their writings widespread attention. Everyone jumped into the debate. Responses ranged from "So what else is new?" to profound shock or to "God is alive because I talked with him this morning." So the belief crisis hit the front page and has been in the news ever since.

In the summer of 1966 the United Church of Christ Board for Homeland Ministries sponsored at Deering, New Hampshire, a conference on the belief crisis. It was attended by highly respected pastors, by representatives of many fields—psychiatry, sociology, physics, journalism, art, biblical studies, and theology—and by church administrators. One of the study groups focused on "The Image of God: Analysis and Assessment of Radical Theology." Its report after ten days of study and discussion was very thoughtful and provocative. The following portion of its report underlines the necessity for the local church to pay attention to this crisis:

> The radical theology has evoked an immediate and widespread response because it reflects the contemporary situation—man's choice and ability to manage his own future. The accompanying belief crisis goes beyond the simple denial of the existence of God to a style that finds either the question itself uninteresting or the word meaningless. In this crisis, many have turned with curiosity and anticipation to the radical theology, while others (including many of the churches) have felt threatened by it. We believe that a serious confrontation with the radical theology is both necessary and helpful, a stimulant toward a needed reinterpretation of the Christian faith; and we welcome the companionship of the radical theologians in the Christian pilgrimage.
>
> Three major figures in the radical theology have emerged as the avant-garde of a larger movement: Thomas J. J. Altizer, William Hamilton, and Paul M. van Buren. We have found these common themes in their thought:
>
> 1. The word and concept of God cease to be useful because the referent is operationally problematic.
>
> 2. The event of Jesus is a central clue to the meaning of human life.
>
> 3. Secularization as the rejection of ontological, metaphysical, and religious frameworks is to be applauded.
>
> 4. Autonomy, understood as man's coming of age through science-technology, the human revolutions of the Very Little

People, and the derivation of ethics from the human context, is to be affirmed.

5. Deep involvement in "the neighbor" questions, optimism about man's future, and radical criticism of the church's failure to give leadership in the human task are in the foreground of the style they propose.

We find the distinctive emphases in the perspective of each theologian to be as follows:

ALTIZER	HAMILTON	VAN BUREN
1. Death of God as event occurring in the divine decision to become incarnate and crucified in Jesus.	1. Death of God: contemporary, and perhaps temporary, through lack of operational effectiveness.	1. The term God is dead through lack of any meaning.
2. Man's role is to affirm and celebrate "deo-suicide."	2. Man's role is to become involved socially, being a man for others.	2. Man's role is to stand on his own feet and help his neighbor.
3. Incarnate Word is present in the world process.	3. The figure of Jesus makes us aware of our social responsibility.	3. In the Easter event, man is grasped by the radical freedom for others seen in Jesus.
4. In history we may anticipate the development of a sacred totality (universal humanity) through spirit.	4. In history we await the possible return of God to be the object of our delight.	4. History is simply ongoing process.
5. Method: mystic-rational apprehension of the coincidence of opposites.	5. Method: empirical-participative.	5. Method: linguistic analysis.

In appraising radical theology, we find that many of its insights and convictions speak significantly to the contemporary situations of both church and the world. Since we are all involved in the belief crisis, we cannot lightly dismiss radical theology, and we must grapple earnestly with what it is saying to us, to the whole church, and to the world.

There followed in the paper a section expressing appreciation for various points of emphasis in the radical theology. This was followed by critical comments and this conclusion:

We have appreciated the seminar process in which we have directly engaged the representatives of radical theology and their critics, and have together forged this statement as a preliminary and tentative step in a crucial inquiry. We have sought to do this in the context of our participation in both the secular ferment of our time and from within the community of faith. We suggest that a similar process might occur in local or regional situations. We feel that the church is strengthened and equipped for its ministry in the world when it wrestles with the significance of radical theology with the aim of fresh commitment to God's purpose in our history.

The question before the local church is not whether there is a belief crisis. Most of us who take our pilgrimage seriously know there is. We know it in our aloneness, when we teach our children, when we talk to our friends, when we seek to witness to our faith. The question before us is: What are we going to do about it?

Chapter 4

The Crisis
of the Local Church

THE 1960's HAVE BEEN troubled years for the local church. During these years it has been subjected to the most stinging attacks it has ever known. And the attacks have come not from the enemies of the church but rather from Christians within the church who, with the battle cries "World," "God's Mission," "New Humanity," "Holy Worldliness," and "New Creation" on their lips, have indicted the local church for failing to change fast enough to minister in a changing world, indicted it for failing to be a revolutionary force in a revolutionary world.

Now, with dozens of books, hundreds of articles, thousands of lectures, thousands of conferences (some of them angry ones), what do we have to say? Where have we come? What have been the results?

We must remind ourselves that this crisis is like every other crisis. It is; and it is an event. Response has to be made. God comes to us clothed in the garments of crisis. The crisis can be for our growth—another opportunity to

move forward with our pilgrim God. So with Paul we need to learn to give thanks for all things, even our discomfiture, even our suffering.

The crisis, long overdue, was postponed during the religious revival of the 1950's. The world is bursting with revolutions; everything has changed as vast institutions have revised old ways of doing things. The local church has remained largely unchanged, all too often speaking the gospel in King James English and trying to make the gospel plain in categories that no longer strike fire with modern, pragmatic, this-worldly man. Somebody, as Pope John XXIII said, had to open a window and let a little fresh air into the church. So he called the Second Vatican Council. The present crisis of the local church in Protestant Christianity has opened plenty of windows, including some in the roof. And the dialogue is far from over. But the breaking open has occurred, and those who have allowed themselves to be broken open can hear a fresh word and do a fresh deed. "He has torn, that he may heal us" (Hos. 6:1).

This has been a time of suffering for many pastors of our churches. No great controversy begins with neat rules carefully laid out. A tense controversy such as has been raging is a vast mixture of many components. It is born of frustration, vision, and hope; it is often laced with lack of sensitivity and unkindness and blindness to another's position. The controversy cuts and bruises without making careful distinctions. The critic wields the ax and lets the chips fall where they may. The pastor of the local church is the first to feel the lash of criticism. He responds with anguish that the church is being downgraded and his work unappreciated. Since he has committed his life to the profession of being a pastor in a local church, a criticism of the local church seems a criticism of him. Understandably, he is often defensive, angry, and resentful. Many pastors have left the profession and are now pursuing others. Some left because they were bitter, others because they became convinced that the local church was irredeemable. Many pastors have moved beyond defensiveness, anger, and resentment and are full participants in the dialogue. They have a real openness to the questions being asked and the word being spoken. Indeed, some of the most helpful, forward-looking words have come from pastors who have led their people into new ways of acting and being. So, hats off to pastors who have coats off to the future, who are staying at their posts, willing to bear the heat of the day! Not too long ago it was a sign of courage and vision to leave the pastorate and, while fully committed to the gospel, seek secular employment. Now, I say, it is a sign of courage and vision to stay and help lead the church through this period of change to a new and faithful stance.

The conversation has probably caused more disruption and uneasiness in congregations than most laymen realize. Many pastors who heard the message of a new age and the call of God to shape life around the needs of this new time and tried to move their church met with deep resistance. Pressure produced resistance and resistance produced anger, not always handled in the best way. Caught between what he believed was a right way to go and a safe way to go, the pastor often fell in the valley of frustration. Laymen need not only to understand the whole crisis but also to understand their pastor so that they will stand alongside of him as he provides leadership in a difficult time.

THE CRITIQUE

Since many laymen are unaware of the main points of the critique of the local church, I will try to review them briefly. Pastors may skip this part; it's all old stuff.

1. The world has changed; the local church has not. God calls the church to minister in the world, the world of

65

the right now. No shape or form is permanently given to the church. The institution serves the God who goes before. Now that the world has changed so radically, the church's failure to change its shape to meet the needs of the changing world mark it as unfaithful.

2. The present structure of the local church is no longer adequate to meet the needs of modern man. Its present form came into being in the Middle Ages when the village was dominant and the church in the center of the village could be in touch with the whole of man's life. The local church is still largely structured around the place of residence, but the average urban working man now spends most of his time away from home, away from the place of residence where the church is set. How significant, ask the critics, is the little time he spends in church?

3. The local church ministers primarily to private life. "Privatism" is the "sin" for which the local church is indicted. The local church is accused of being fundamentally inward-looking. This is true whether we are talking about the revivalist with his "private savior," or the peace-of-mind cult, or the weltschmerz of the existentialist. Furthermore, the church is seen essentially as a "come" structure with an appeal to personal needs: "Come to be saved," "Come to find forgiveness," "Come to find the strength for your life," "Get free of your personal burdens, overcome sickness and bereavement, marital problems, and loneliness." The local church ministers primarily to the family, upon which it is almost entirely centered. But the family has given up many of its responsibilities; the school, the gang, and the culture in general shape the values and norms of the children and young people. The church, quite self-consciously centering on the family, seems unable really to make much difference.

4. There is a failure to establish a depth relation with the people who are members of the church. The members

know one another only in superficial ways; they covenant together to love one another and to pray for one another, but they know one another only on the surface. Since one in every five families moves every year, this superficiality is increased.

5. The local church is called to assume the shape of its servant Lord but instead is shaped by the society it serves; and, being shaped by the society, the local church acts always for its institutional well-being instead of following the servant Lord in faithfulness. The local church coheres so closely to the society it serves that it is swallowed up by the society.

6. We are called to be present not only at the weak points of man's existence but at his strong points as well. But the local church is separated from the great centers of power in our times. The vast complexes of industry, government, the military establishment, the communications media, and the movements for social change such as the civil rights movement are the shakers and the movers. The church, while present here and there, is still largely absent.

7. The local church is not involved in the great issues of our time. Its failure to influence the thinking of men relative to the great moral issues of our time is apparent. Again, prime influence of the church is in the private sector, not the public sector. And, say the critics, massive evidence shows that the member of the local church has no unique style of life to distinguish him from any other person. His thinking, his values, his ethics, his vision apparently are no different from that of the nonchurch member in our culture.

8. The local church attempts to domesticate the God who goes before us. God's mission is to and for the world. He intends the salvation of the world. He is present where newness is breaking, where man is breaking free from chains that bind him; he is present wherever humanization is going on. It is God's mission; the mission of the church

67

is to participate in that mission. Hence the slogan of the
renewers, reformers, and radicals, God/World/Church, not
God/Church/World.

9. If the church of Jesus Christ is involved where the
people are, where the suffering is, where the power is, and
where the issues are, then new forms must arise. Society is
now differentiated; the church must now differentiate its
forms. If it is going to be where the action is, it can no
longer rely upon a single form to carry out this important
work. New forms must appear—on ski slopes, in coffee-
houses, amusement centers, night ministries, and inner
cities, in the centers of industrial power, in the communications industry, in storefront churches and house churches.
We need new shapes of ministry to the metropolis and new
shapes of ministry by the layman within the context of his
profession. New forms of ministry need to emerge where
the great issues are being hammered out and where significant decisions which shape the future are being made.

10. The local church is called to be a community that
demonstrates to the world the character of shalom, God's
intent for all mankind. Instead many local churches practice discrimination in regard to race and serve only one
class of people. Thus, they fail to be a sign of the new age.
The church fits too neatly the culture all around it. What
should be dysfunctional and controversial is tame and con-
forming. The church looks and behaves like any other institution seeking worldly success.

11. The failure of unity on the local level is shameful
and a disgrace before the world. The world searches and
longs for unity; there is tremendous need for a personal
basis of morality. And the church, which is to be a sign of
the unity of all mankind, still spends its time in costly com-
petition, perpetuating historical feuds and silly divisions
that no longer make any sense.

12. Because worship in the local church is detached

from the agonies and issues of the world, to that extent it is inauthentic. It is trying to reach modern man with archaic words and concepts. In the midst of a massive belief crisis, man needs more than archaic forms and concepts.

13. The forms of the life of the church should depend on function. They should be designed to facilitate locating and participating in the mission of God. They should effectuate rather than hinder the discovery of and cooperation in the work of God in the world. The content of the church's ministry should be shaped by the world's agenda and be the continuation of Jesus' ministry. The main clue to the whereabouts of Jesus' ministry in the world is the servant style.

14. Authentic theological reflection can go on only in the midst of involvement. A living theology for our time, therefore, can only be shaped from the involvement context.

15. The laity are not assistants to the clergy, justifying themselves by helping the church. Rather the clergy, through their theological specialty, help the laity, who are set in the midst of the world.

WHAT SHALL WE SAY?

First of all, let's try to hear these criticisms, really hear them, let them sink in. Actual dialogue can proceed only on the basis of hearing—real hearing—and response. All of us who love the local church in general, and one local church in particular, need to hear and respond. Any local church that finds the way of faithfulness in these times will grapple with the judgments and questions such as have been raised and will make response not only in answer but also in new ways of acting and being. Some of the criticisms and judgments will be proven wrong; still others are being abrogated because of the new life now emerging. There is no end to the creativity possible when man has seen a new vision and covenants to move into new country, and many local churches have seen this vision.

In the meantime some things seem clear. Let us define our great assets, and let us see in these strengths the call of God to be good stewards of what he has given.

1. The institutional church as we know it is presently structured for mission with its primary financial dependence on the local church. With the exception of some boards and agencies that are endowed, the support of the wider mission is heavily dependent upon the local church. There is nothing to assure us that this is the way it will always be, but this is the way it is now. This function must be considered not a burden, but a means of participating in the wider mission of God.

2. The primary recruitment for the Christian life goes on through the local church. Here is where witness is made, where new Christians come into being, babies are baptized, children are confirmed, covenants are made. Here children and adults are incorporated into the memory of the church and made one with the pilgrim people of God.

3. Here in the local church the nurturing process is carried out through Christian education and it is here that Christians are equipped for mission in the world.

4. It is in the local church that the public worship of God is carried out Sunday after Sunday.

5. The local church ministers to persons in their private world. The dialogue going on now speaks the word private almost with a slur. This is because the passion in the dialogue is for the world filled with unjust structures that imprison the person, gross injustice that needs to be righted, poverty, racial discrimination, war. We need to sense this passion, but at the same time we must see the local church's magnificent opportunity to minister to the private world. It is a world of utmost importance and, though sometimes we

talk about them as "hatching, matching, and dispatching," the areas of marriage, birth, childhood, adolescence, decision-making, suffering, mourning, and dying are areas of ultimate importance. The local church has entry into this world. I know of no agency in so favorable a position to minister to people in their need.

6. The local church exists as a sign of shalom to the world. The difference between the church and the world is that the church is to be a sign of what God intends; it is to be a representative community, a community that exists in behalf of the whole world. The very way in which its people relate, the love they express to one another, the deeds they do become this sign. "Behold how these Christians love one another," was one of the important means of conversion in the early days of the church.

7. The local church exists in a community. There is human need all around the church, all around and in the homes where people live. There are important human problems in which the church can and must be involved in the person of its members as well as with its own institutional life. Beyond this we must see the metropolis as the real setting of the church and we must find new ways of planning for participation in God's mission with other churches in the metropolis.

8. We have many more people on mission than seems apparent. We do not yet know how to use this involvement of the laity in the world, both for the sake of those served and for those who think about the shape of the church.

But we have no reason to rest on our laurels. The money that is raised for use in the mission of God beyond the local church is pitifully small, so small that Vice President Humphrey, addressing the General Assembly of the National Council of Churches, pointed out the great disparity between the words of the church and its deeds. Most of the money is spent right at home keeping the institution alive.

In our recruitment of members we do not keep up with the population growth in this country, and the persons received into the church are apparently poorly trained for the new life in the church (that is, if we can trust the numerous sociological studies that test for persons' knowledge of the Bible, church history, ethical imperatives, and nature and function of the church). Evidently our nurturing process rounds out too early and we have much to learn concerning how that nurture can best go on.

Our worship is still in old forms, many of our hymns are quite archaic, and even our prayers are voiced in categories that do not reflect the new science and the whole set of components that have changed the ways in which men look at life.

Ministry in the private world is still done largely by the pastor, for we have not yet learned an appropriate style in this new age whereby the members may truly minister to one another.

So our work is cut out for us. There is plenty of potentiality, and plenty of problems.

SOME THINGS WE CAN DO

1. We cannot do everything, so let us do something. The job is vast. Society is too differentiated for one form of the church's life to carry almost the whole responsibility, so let us find out what the local church can do well and concentrate on those areas. I have listed the following: financial support of the total mission; recruitment of new Christians; nurture and equipment of Christians through worship and study and involvement; a ministry to persons in crisis; being a sign of God's shalom, his intention for the whole world through the way we love one another and

the way in which we minister in the community where we are. This community, large or small, is a part of the whole metropolis and we must take this into account.

2. Let us support the emergence of new forms in the varied sectors of our society and at the many points of human need and power. The church at other times was able to recognize this. Many of our national instrumentalities and agencies were new forms in their day, so we are not the first generation called upon to recognize the need.

3. Let's get off the defensive and start to work updating our ways of acting and being. We need to give up the naïve idea that somewhere there are a few enemies who are causing all the troubles and if they could just be eliminated then things would go back to normal. The world has changed, and we have to rise to meet it and shape our lives and institutions accordingly. Defensiveness leads nowhere but backward.

4. Let's face the fact that denominationalism is dying. There is really no biblical basis or good commonsense reason to keep it alive. We will have denominations with us for a long time, but the "we are the greatest" aspect of denominationalism and the competitiveness engendered must be allowed a dignified death. Denominationalism served a purpose in its time, but it has fulfilled its function and deserves a long, long rest—forever, as a matter of fact. We now must seek ways of planning for mission with all Christians in one place.

5. Let us remember that we are first of all a people, the pilgrim people of God. Our institutions are not ultimate; they are simply instruments by which we can fulfill the tasks God gives us to do. Let us bring our pilgrim spirit to bear upon the task ahead of us, the task of bringing our local church to the shape and style whereby it can minister in an age that is new.

Chapter 5

Facing Change
and Conflict

CHANGE IS NATURAL to all of life and to all institutions; it is a twin to conflict. Individual growth and progress in institutions involve the facing and resolving of conflicts.

If we are going to take seriously the updating of the local church, we must be willing to grapple with change— its theological, psychological, and sociological implications. We have to be sensitive as to how to effect change with minimum damage. But we cannot engage in updating the church without engendering conflict. We must not presume that important and significant changes can occur in the church simply because we will them. Something needs to change in *us* as well. Some turning has to occur.

CHANGE

In the preface of this book I referred to notable World Council of Churches studies on "The Missionary Structure of the Congregation." Study groups on five continents have been doing distinguished work in attempting to clarify a theology of mission for a world in change. I commend most strongly to you a single volume containing both the Western European and the North American section report.[1]

One of the Western European members, Hans Schmidt of Hamburg, Germany, has written in such a compact way and so beautifully about change that I want to borrow his words. They say clearly what I think needs to be heard by us Christians as we struggle with the problem of change.

1. It is not the task with which Christians are faced today merely to recognize that the world in which they live is no longer the world of 1920. Nor are they called simply to discard beloved conceptions and entrenched customs in order to make themselves at home in a changed world. The task reaches further.

2. We shall have to face up to the fact that change is part of our situation in the world and that, as far as we can see, there will never be stable conditions anymore.

3. We shall have to understand how in the midst of a continually changing world to keep faith, to exercise love, and to walk humbly, to the praise of God and to the pleasing of men.

4. Through the biblical witness the world is opened up to us as the field of service for faith combined with hope and love. The biblical witness proclaims that God opens up ways even in the desert . . . in order that in the places of apparent hopelessness fountains of joy spring up (Psalm 84:6). It is to be expected of the Christians that they trust these promises and accordingly involve themselves in the world (cf. Romans 12:1 f.). For they are to confess and witness that all of God's promises have found their Yes in Jesus Christ (2 Corinthians 1:20) and are, therefore, available to us as our heritage (Galatians 4—5).

5. The orders of the church, therefore, should be much more like a marching order than a camping order (cf. Hebrews 13:12-14). It would be dangerous for us to become guilty of confusions, to confuse the "God of peace" with the "God of order" (cf. 1 Corinthians 14:33), to speak of "hope in God" and to mean "hope in stable conditions," to speak of "God's faithfulness" and thereby try to save the status quo instead of discerning the oncoming.

6. God is a God of Abraham, Isaac, and Jacob; he is not to be likened to the God of the fathers but he is a God of the grandfather, the father, and the son, a God of the generations who calls himself a people to walk with him. God is the creator who elects persons for the purpose of involvement in the world as the history of the covenant; people called and liberated in the service of God to take co-responsibility for the world.

7. Jesus Christ is the man who has truly fulfilled the office of man in a changing world; the firstborn among many brothers (Romans 8:29), the second Adam (Romans 5:12 ff.), the Son of God, obedient unto death on the cross, in whom God himself spoke when in dealing with man and world he totally conformed to the will of God for man and world. In him it has been ultimately revealed what God intends for man and the world: that he has intentions of peace! Therein Jesus as the Christ is the Lord of the world and of his congregation. Thus the congregation lives from the task to discern Christ as the Lord of the changing world. For this, witnesses are sought who through their witness liberate men in the world for their God-given promising worldly service.[2]

The local congregation. Practically every major institution in our culture has changed so much since World War II that it is hardly recognizable. This includes banking institutions, major industries, schools, and colleges. Thoughtful and competent leaders have engaged experts from a wide variety of disciplines in order to effect this change. They have spared no expense in toil or money in order to shape their institutions to serve the needs of this new time. The church is one of the few institutions that have been slow in getting the message that the age is new and requires radical adjustments. Of course, many laymen and leaders have known that the age was new, but whenever they have sought to effect change they have run into stone walls of resistance. One of the reasons there is massive unrest in the churches today is that efforts to update the institutions have encountered such mighty opposition.

Why? Look at the wide variety of feelings, ideas, experiences, and ages in a local church. The local church is like the bumblebee: according to all the laws of aerodynamics it can't fly, but it does. The local church, however, is flying much too slowly today.

Unique among voluntary organizations, the local church spans the generations from infancy to old age. After a young person is confirmed he presumably has a voice thereafter in the affairs of the church. Persons who make up the membership of the local congregation come from a broad spread of denominations. A pastor often finds that those from denominations other than his own outnumber those who grew up in his particular denomination. Almost every pastor finds in his church today persons of Roman Catholic background, from Pentecostal churches, from high and low churches, and from conservative and liberal backgrounds; increasingly pastors find in their congregations persons of Jewish background. The members come from all over the country and often from all over the world. The transportation revolution has radically altered the background and composition of the local church. The homogeneity which could be counted on only yesterday now no longer exists.

Confronted by this heterogeneous background, will members not surmise that their experiencing of the meanings of the church will be quite various? It almost seems that each member has his own unique picture in his head about what a church is and what a pastor should be! As to the latter, most of us have had a pastor who really turned us on. Then he left, or we moved, but inside there remains a warm glow about him; and, when we are at odds with another pastor, that memory glows in the dark. No one else will ever match that picture because in many ways it is fantasy. Others have a picture in their heads of a church in which "things were done right"—meaning a way in which things are *not now* being done. Add to this the fact that we church members are different psychologically. No matter how much new learning comes to us, or even how much therapy, chances are we will continue to make our own automatic responses to change and to the need for change.

As a final complicating factor, many today see the church as a haven in a world of change. Everything around them has changed, so they have a vital need to feel that there is *one* place that has *not* changed, a place that is "just as it was when mother and father were alive and I was a little child. Everything changes, except the church. Like God, it is changeless." The mere fact that this picture in the head goes against all history does not make any difference. All through the ages, the church has changed to meet changing times. Of course its updating has often been belated, but it has changed. Yet this fantasy of an immutable church is an enduring one and a real impediment in the life and mission of the church today. We have to take into account this picture of the church as surely as we have to take into account that person who thinks that all change is good, who will gladly pull the whole house down on top of him to produce change. So when we talk about changing something in the church, we are up against something formidable!

But do we have to think of this wide variety of responses only in negative terms? Is it possible that this increased variety in the church might be a very positive factor? Surely we can learn a great deal from one another if we can find ways of opening ourselves to others and sharing what is deep inside—the wealth of meanings and experiencings and learnings we have to give to others. All kinds of skills are represented in a congregation, and yet at times they

78

seem bottled up, unavailable to God and man. We make noises in the presence of others, but fail to communicate. We talk about love, reconciliation, and forgiveness—yet at times the local church seems to incarnate just the opposite when it "solves" its problems in human relations by a shameful violation of common decency.

What's the matter? We must not evade the fact of alienation. The Bible speaks of this crucial factor in the life of man—man's alienation from himself, from others, from nature, from God. The problem is all the more acute in modern man. So massive and complex have grown the structures in which we all live that we are threatened with a sense of futility and powerlessness. Our estrangement from one another in differing degrees is at the root of our loneliness, anxiety, frustration, insecurity, and hopelessness, our feelings of worthlessness, mistrust, boredom, and fear. By failing to act responsibly toward one another we are alienated. This alienation is perpetuated by dishonesty, self-centeredness, false communication, myths about others, and a lack of integrity resulting from inconsistency between belief and behavior. So the church, which speaks so much of reconciliation, love, and forgiveness, becomes instead a place of unforgiveness, stereotyped thinking, deceit, and dishonesty. Oftentimes we find ourselves hooked and ashamed, not knowing how to extricate ourselves.

In our best moments we know what's the matter. We know that it is not enough to embrace a truth intellectually; we must live it. It is not enough simply to talk a truth, we must *become* a truth. It is not enough to tell good news, we must be good news to one another. Strangely, this leads us to the subject of conflict, for it is impossible to overcome alienation and experience growth without the creative handling of conflict.

CONFLICT

When we think of conflict, most of us automatically respond negatively. The pictures in our heads related to the word are those of hostility, war, disorder, aggression, violence, wounds, and somebody's losing. There is, of course, one side of us that associates conflict with sports, which is a positive association. But, by and large, most of our responses would test out negative. Yet we know that conflict is a necessary aspect of existence. In fact, social scientists have little difficulty showing that it is through the creative resolution of conflict that we grow as human beings and fulfill organizational functions.

Some propositions about conflict.
1. Conflict occurs in the local church because in some way we are bound together; we are interdependent. If we were not so bound that our actions affect one another, conflict could not occur.
2. Conflict occurs because we care. If we did not care we would not make costly emotional response to what is going on. Often people in the local church who are in conflict share a very deep relationship.
3. Conflict grows out of the different needs we bring and the different values we have. It frequently emerges when decisions have to be made in regard to the direction that the church should take in its life and mission.

I have already spoken of the tragedy that now and then accompanies church conflict. This occurs when members, not open about facing the true reasons for the conflict, delay overt response to it until high temperature melts the evasions. Churchly types are past masters at uttering sweet pleasantries in the presence of subterranean conflict. Because the conflict is hidden and not openly resolved, its power becomes demonically destructive. Under conditions of avoidance and noncommunication, unrealistic versions of the conflict obscure reality. Most specialists in the subject agree that conflict is inherent in human life and that we have to accept it as an important part of human relations. This does not excuse ignoring it or drifting passively in its presence or rejoicing in the destruction it often causes. It means that we must develop ways of handling conflict other than those of denial and evasion and explosion.

The creative handling of conflict. If the world has changed as radically as I have asserted, if in the light of these changes the local church needs to be updated, how can church members be helped to face this need and to move to a more relevant stance in the present world? This question is asked in the light of the varieties of persons, backgrounds, and experiencings in each local church.

First, we need to confess that the problem cannot be faced at all without conflict. A full recognition of this from the start is extremely important. Different feelings, different pictures in the head, different value structures, different idea systems are going to run into one another head on.

Second, each party to the conflict must accept the right of the other parties to their feelings, pictures in the head, values, and ideas. One of the important components in personhood is the right to think and feel as we think and feel.

Third, we cannot proceed to the resolution of serious problems without some kind of trust. We come to trust, not because we are told that we should, but rather because another person shows himself trustworthy. To be trustworthy is to be honest; and in the study or the resolution of problems, one is called to be honest not only about ideas but about feelings as well.

81

Fourth, we must courageously proceed to the realistic location of the problem or problems and then make careful, intelligent analysis of the parts. We must study the problem, debate the issues honestly and with open mind and heart, then imaginatively project different solutions and make tentative decisions relative to them. Finally, we must experiment with new ways of acting and being and must build evaluation into all that we do.

The way a local church goes about facing the necessity of change, then, is basically no different from that of any other organization which creatively faces its need for updating.

THE PILGRIM CHURCH AND CHANGE

But the church is not simply another institution. Despite the fact that its members are made up of many different backgrounds and many different psychological types and many different worlds of experiences, the local church is a part of the one pilgrim people of God. Although it adds to the history and the story, it does not invent that history or make up that story. The church does not belong to itself or to the people who make up its membership; it is a part of a stream of history-making, part of a culture that is rich in meaning, related to a pilgrim God who calls a pilgrim people. The local church therefore has roots and is duty-bound to discern them, thus learning from the vast wisdom of church history. There is a faithful stance implicit in that history, a pilgrim stance still related to the encountering of God, the seeing of a vision, the hearing of a call to go into a new country and live not for one's own benefit but in order to bless the world. In other words, the local church is a part of the pilgrim people of God and does not exist primarily for those who are in it but for those who are *not* in it.

82

The attempt on the part of the local church to come to grips with a changed world is to encounter God in the process, the God who ever and again calls his people to take the risks of leaving the familiar and of dwelling in a new country, believing that he who calls them will be with them. The pilgrim perspective, which sees change in positive terms, sees the future as that into which we enter with faith and trust.

We cannot engage in the pilgrim's process unless we ourselves are willing to be changed. This is another way of saying that we are willing to grow, that we are willing to allow pictures in our head to change, that we are willing to give up an idea if we are convinced that there is a better one. It means that we are willing to allow a new vision of what we are and what we intend for both ourselves and the church to become a reality. For the new day God needs new men and women with a new vision and a new trust in the God of yesterday, today, and tomorrow.

Chapter 6

Planning for Change

MANY OF THE LAITY are tired of facing and adjusting to change. To compete successfully today the institutions in which they work have had to alter their processes and structures. Tired of the resultant insecurities, these laity want to avoid such disruption in their churches. They may not voice it in just this way, but they like to keep alive the fantasy that the church does not change, that it is the same "yesterday, today, and forever." And they think that they have biblical ground for this notion. They are not aware that they have confused the church with God. They want the church to be a haven of rest, not just one more place that reminds them of the changing world and its problems.

In contrast, many clergy have realized that the world has changed radically, the church has not. They preach about a new world being born, and they urge the need for change in the life of the church. This irritates the above-mentioned laity and makes them nervous. Little wonder that the more aggressive fight back: "Let's get rid of this gadfly. He drives me to distraction with all his talk about change!" Soon a move is under way to urge the pastor to seek a "greater challenge" elsewhere.

But other laity have got another message: "The world has changed radically; the church has not." They make some pastors and some laity nervous because they keep saying, "Unless the church changes its style, unless it begins to live in this present world instead of yesterday, I'm leaving. I can spend my time and money better somewhere else."

But some clergy have not got the message. Emotionally, if not intellectually, they respond as though the Bible were written in timeless English, as though the form of the church in the time of King James were given for all times, as though they could best get their directions for living today by looking at the past. They are perfectly at home singing hymns and saying prayers whose world view no longer conforms to what we know about the universe and whose ideas about the community around them are still informed by a concept of village life. Laymen who are really alive to the changes in the world and the call of God to his people today make such clergy nervous.

Do these categories seem familiar? Perhaps you found yourself somewhere in this description of the church's present reactions to change. Many of us who love the local church are restless. Are you? What shall we do? Let's face it, getting rid of one more minister isn't going to solve the problem. Nor is choosing up sides in the congregation for one more power struggle. And what is to be gained by walking out of the church either for conservative or for liberal reasons? Is the church a club to which we pay dues and retain the right to quit when things don't go our way?

Our churches are restless today. Anxiety is high among the clergy; pastors change churches far too often. Many in the church are quietly angry; many more are unfulfilled.

An earthquake has hit our culture. Should we be surprised that many things are set atilt and many people are shocked and upset? But what shall we *do?* How do we as mature people solve the problems now thrust at us—indeed, assigned to us by God? Don't the many fragments of the church's life have to find one another, hear one another, and overcome the alienation occasioned by different ways of perceiving and relating to contemporary realities?

WHAT DO WE NEED?

The crisis in the local church today is so severe that we are called upon not only to update our thinking but also to find new ways of functioning. Here are some critical needs that face us.

1. Just as other institutions of our society have had to respond to a radically changed world, so must the church. The fact that we are late in getting at this task only makes the imperative stronger.

2. Not only must we respond to changes which have already occurred, we must also update our way of functioning as a church so as to take into account the truth that change is especially characteristic of this new age and that we therefore need a flexible style of operation.

3. We need a way of clarifying our goals. The lack of clarity in the local church concerning objectives is a scandal. We must become aware that our goals and objectives emerge from our identity as God's pilgrim people. We do not start from scratch in deciding what the church is; we are part of a particular stream of history-making, a culture, a people who live in dynamic relationship with God. Our objectives should emerge consciously out of our understanding of who God is, what he is doing here and now, and how we in our particular churches are related to his

mission. This is our theological task, a task belonging to the whole people of God, not simply to pastors.

4. We must find ways to involve a maximum number of people in the churches in study, dialogue, and decision-making. We must discover how the many skills represented in the membership of the congregation can be released to inform our ways of being and doing.

5. We must perceive accurately the world we live in. I call this "situation definition." Unless the world we live in is adequately discerned, a local church cannot function effectively as a people.

6. We need to learn the facts about ourselves. This involves some form of disciplined self-study. We need to be clear about our identity, our mission, and our objectives. If we are clear about the situation; that is, how well we are doing what we intend to do or, more painfully put, how well our deeds conform with our words, we have honest and intelligent ground for planning.

7. We need to learn whether we have the appropriate structures to fulfill our objectives as the pilgrim people of God.

8. We need a way to work at the crisis of the local church in such a way as to dig appropriate channels. A river without banks lacks power. In the changed world of today the local church is in many ways without banks and consequently lacks power. We must find out what the inherent limitations of the local church are and what self-chosen limitations—"banks"—are needed to move toward decided goals.

9. We are a long way from knowing how to make full use of the vast, latent power of the laity.

10. We must find a built-in style of continuous re-examination of our life. It is not enough for the local

church to take an occasional look at itself. The world changes, time moves, nothing is constant. We need to know what is going on and to what degree we are fulfilling our intended aims.

THE PLANNING PROCESS

I contend that the planning process, now growing rapidly in theory and expertise, can be an important response to the needs just delineated. No rational person lives without doing some kind of planning. Planning is part of the process of human life—means whereby man faces real situations, creatively imagines the future, seeks ways to fulfill his visions. Planning, inseparable from the total life-process, is goal-clarification and the defining of means to fulfill goals in a dynamically changing world.

Most of us who try to plan intelligently follow something of this process: we define the problem; we read and study the best sources; we consult experts; we define issues; we discern possible new shapes of action or being; we make decisions; we act; we evaluate; and we celebrate. All of us can be helped to plan more effectively by persons who have skills in planning and the capacity to stand alongside us as we learn. Many of us have had someone stand in this relation to us, helping us shape painful questions more clearly, clarify our visions, give sharper expression to a particular goal, and think about alternative ways of achieving it.

The local church is not a single person but is many persons bound together as a people through a shared covenant. But just as a person can be helped in planning his life through a process of study, experimentation, and reflection, so can a church. No one can do the planning for us as persons; to do so would violate our personhood. So also the local church must do its own planning. But it can be helped. Through the planning process it can come to face the truth about its world and itself, and thus move from haphazard and wasteful use of its energies and resources.

Can we learn from the business world? We church members can and should learn from the business world, which since World War II has been busy developing and utilizing planning processes. Today billions of dollars are spent on research, an integral aspect of planning. Business has acquired skills and insights from the behavioral sciences, such as sociology, psychology, economics, and anthropology. While churches need to learn everything they can from business and from the behavioral sciences, churches are not businesses.

True, churches as institutions with properties and salaried staff are duty-bound to learn everything they can from the world of business; there is no excuse for careless procedures in money and personnel. But a church errs when it sees itself in terms of the business model. As the pilgrim people of God, a church will be wiser to use the political or educational or communications model as more nearly fitting the local-church realities. Undoubtedly our assumptions that the local church is a business have been unconscious, but they are present, and all the more powerful for being unconscious. The business model often determines behavior and also evaluative procedures. Yet we are called to a qualitative existence, whereas business measurements are quantitative; we are called to faithfulness, not to success. And, no matter how efficient we may become, however successful in getting more members and more money, we shall be woefully unfaithful if our primary goals are statistical.

The church must design its own planning methods, using the best it can borrow from the business world combined with methods that fit the special requirements of its mission and structures.

The planning process of the local church. This is not the place to present a detailed picture of what presently is known about the local church and the planning process. Others have done this already, and their material is available. My hope is to interest you enough so that you will take advantage of the important aids available through the National Council of Churches and your own denomination. I give only this warning: Sustained concern and scholarship in this area are quite recent and, even after you have the best material available, much will still depend on your own imagination and creativity.

There are no shortcuts to turning the congregation toward the world. Ahead of us is the hard task of grasping more firmly our identity, appraising rightly our situation, clarifying our goals, facing our real problems, delineating how we intend to participate in God's mission, finding appropriate ways of investing our resources, and building adequate evaluative procedures into whatever we do. We can come to know the joy of faithful action. We can know that we are not alone, that he who calls us has gone before us and will meet us as we move into the distinctive mission he has for us as a congregation.

A DEFINITION OF CHURCH PLANNING

Planning in the local church is the disciplined, continuous process whereby we as the pilgrim people of God come to understand our world, our identity, and our specific part as we participate in God's mission. This "specific part" or "distinctive mission" is always a step-by-step process of action, reflection on the action, and a revised program of action in the light of the reflection.

The word disciplined here means that planning must be undertaken by responsible governing groups, that the process must be clearly delineated and understood broadly within the congregation. Appropriate machinery must be set up whereby disciplined study may go on, policy become shaped, new action be imaginatively projected, decision-making procedures be agreed on, and new forms of action emerge. Into this process it is necessary to build adequate evaluative procedures.

"Continuous" means that planning is not just something that happens once and is then over. To be alive means to plan. To be an institution means that some kind of planning is always going on. The question is, what kind of planning? Careful planning must be built into the life-style of a church, and the steps in planning must be seen not as rungs on a ladder with a top but as a continuous unending flow.

Identity as "the pilgrim people of God" is crucial. We are, first of all, a people. Our institutional forms are only tents and should be highly flexible and movable. How the local church conceives itself is crucial to its planning process and is the ground upon which everything else flows. The pilgrim people's planning should come naturally to us who sense ourselves caught up in the greatest long-range plan there is—God's intention for his whole creation.

The phrase "understand our world" is critical in all planning. Related to "our identity" is our belief that God loves the whole world and is carrying out his mission in the world. Since it is our task to join him, we must know something about that world of the here and now. History does not stand still; we cannot understand the present simply by understanding the past. History moves not in a circular fashion but in a linear fashion. As Christians, we believe that the world is moving toward fulfillment. The people of the local congregation must ever and again understand their world in terms of who they are as God's pilgrim people. Knowledge of God and man must be brought together in the life of the church.

"Our specific part" in "God's mission" means that, unless our planning eventuates in specific ways of acting and being, it is in vain. We are called as the pilgrim people of God, as the followers of Jesus Christ, to be in the world for others, to have a pro-existence for all men. Hence, we are called to act. Planning is action-oriented and the planning process clarifies and informs our actions.

There is a certain kind of woolly thinking which assumes that the church should *not* act. But people today are deeply disturbed about the church's inaction. Perry L. Norton, a city planner, says:

To be sure, much Christian thinking concerning the good society (i.e., Utopia) is transhistorical and eschatological in nature. This poses for many laymen, including myself, a real problem. What in fact are we supposed to conclude when we read (with monotonous repetition) of graft, corruption and cheating, and lying? What *shall* we conclude when Michael Harrington so devastatingly exposes the existence of the other America? That this is simply another manifestation of sinful man and let it go at that? I have had clergymen tell me (in an effort to be reassuring, I am sure) that man is intrinsically sinful and that I should not, therefore, be unduly distressed at the inequities that derive from this sinfulness. But I *am* distressed. And as I look into this social mirror, it occurs to me that there are others who are also perturbed that their formal religious experience does not speak very precisely to the conditions with which they, as whole persons, must somehow come to grips.

Planning is a way of responding to changes that have already occurred. Too, it is a process whereby change, which is constantly occurring, may be addressed. But it is also *a* way of making things happen. The church is not simply a passive reactor to whatever happens. It is also the initiator of change.[1]

"Participation in God's mission" means the mission is God's; it is the redemption of the whole world. Our task is to participate in this mission, to join God in the world he loves. The separate aims of local churches emerge from this center. Each congregation is under orders to discover and fulfill God's specific assignments where people are lonely, searching for meaning, hungry, blind, lame. This mission means working with God wherever man longs for peace. It means working with God to destroy whatever cripples and imprisons the spirit of man.

BASIC COMPONENTS IN PLANNING

1. *Dialogue is central.* Here, in a disciplined way, members of differing points of view take one another seriously, not simply for their own sakes but for the sake of the mission of God and the common tasks radiating therefrom. Each brings to the other not only his feelings and his fears but his best thinking and his hopes. It is a tragic fact that people in most local churches meet one another on superficial levels, speaking primarily in areas where there is known agreement and avoiding areas of deepest threat and most tender meanings. Wherever Christians shrink from the disciplined and loving task of dialogue, there the church is weaker, the mission is sinned against, the ministries are undiscerned and unfulfilled.

2. *The emergence of community.* Planning is not a lonely, unilateral affair; it should involve the whole church. When engaged in a disciplined fashion, it will strengthen true community in the local church. "We" becomes strong, "they" fades away, and we come to know our life together in Christ.

3. *Those engaged in planning must be willing to recognize change and conflict as normal, healthy aspects of existence.* Am I willing to confront and respond to change

93

and enter into conflict with those who respond to the world in ways different from mine?

4. *Planning must take into account the whole mission of the whole people of God.* Careful attention must be paid not only to what the local church can do but also to what it cannot do and what therefore it must support other forms of ministry in doing in order that the mission of the church may be whole.

5. *Planning should be done with other churches.* Denominationalism is dying. As spirit and as institution it is inadequate to serve the world being born. Planning, accordingly, should not be done on a competitive basis, but in cooperation with a view to a full ministry in each place. The primary concern of planning is not competitive success but a total ministry that can be carried out to the total community, local and larger.

6. *A willingness to experiment.* Planning requires that those who engage in it dare experiment, knowing that to experiment is to take the chance of failing.

PLANNING AS A PILGRIM PROCESS

The characteristics of pilgrimage outlined in chapter 1 are applicable to the planning process in the local church.

1. *Encounter with God.* The planning process involves facing reality through research and self-study, encountering persons in depth, deep concern for the needs of others, decision-making, and acting. Precisely in these areas we encounter the pilgrim God who calls us and says, "Go."

2. *Vision.* In the process of planning, the operational vision (not necessarily the vision we have sung about or prayed about or talked about) appears. The operational vision is the one by which we are actually living, the one in the light of which our real decisions are made. The planning process is a means whereby we may clarify our vision, share it with others, learn from them, perhaps catch anew

that vision which Jesus Christ incarnated and which has burned as a flame in the life of saints, prophets, and martyrs in all ages.

3. *Openness to the future.* This pilgrim quality spells risk. All who participate deeply in the planning process are like Abraham, who "went out, not knowing where he was to go." Planning is open-ended; we do not know where we are going to come out. If we knew ahead of time, we would not have to engage in the process! Planning entails risking our lives. Some churches may even find that they must cease to exist as separate entities. For others it may mean a radical change in the way in which the life of the local church is carried on. In still others it may mean a radical change in structure. But without risk we cannot discern and fulfill our mission, cannot really be present to the needs of this world in the name of Christ.

4. *Living in tents.* The spirit of all true planning is a willingness to abandon whatever no longer fulfills the mission function, a willingness to act out the truth that institutional shapes and forms are no more than means to ends, so that when better shapes and forms can be found they are utilized and the old ones abandoned. To live in tents means that we hold with a light grip all institutional forms. Only God is ultimate. To cling to dysfunctional forms would be idolatry. We search always for a better way to shape our life as a servant people.

5. *Living for others.* The church exists for the sake of the world. The planning process is but a means whereby we probe the problem of how to be present in the world for the sake of the whole world.

6. *Faith and hope.* Our faith and hope is in the God who goes before us. He is present in the planning process. We participate in it in the confidence that he who goes before us will lead us in a right way.

Chapter 7

Thinking, Acting, Reflecting, Celebrating

I HAVE NOT FORGOTTEN for whom I am writing this book: the core group people in the local church. Many of you are aware of the tensions and problems in your churches during this time of turning, but I hope you do not see the new age with its changes and uncertainties as a time of despair. It is a time when we can experience the joy of a fresh situation, a time when great things are happening and greater things can happen, a time of radical change when we are called to radical faithfulness. The years just past have been years of struggle. The days ahead will not offer less struggle, but are bright with hope for those who are broken open and able to hear a fresh word. Only those who have borne the pain of the truth about themselves are open also to hear the good news. You are open enough to read this book; this occasions *my* hope! Now I want to begin to draw together some ideas which have appeared in this book and to make some simple recommendations as to how your local church may greet this new day with faith and joy rather than with fear and despair.

A PILGRIM THEOLOGY

I have said that we who are members of the local church need to see ourselves as a particular people in history, as a special stream of history-making. To be a people dynamically related to the living God is not the same thing as to belong to an institution. We are a people loved by God as are all peoples, and we have a distinctive style of life, a special witness to make in deed and word. Our style is a pilgrim style of encounter with God, of vision, of openness and risk, of pro-existence and faith and hope. Our witness is to live the life and ministry of Jesus Christ in the world, and the word we speak is the word of God's love and of our love for God and man.

At different times in history different aspects of our faith have come to the center of the stage, to be seen with great clarity and heard with fresh understanding. The aspect I believe should get central attention today is what I have been calling "pilgrim theology." It goes something like this: God loves all mankind and his redemptive work is understood in relation to the world in its totality. The arena of his saving action is history. We Christians understand our life in relationship to the God of history, who calls us to assume our responsibility as partners with him in history-making. The mission of the God of exodus and Easter is redemption, setting man free from whatever shackles and imprisons him. God is carrying out his mission in the midst of history, and he calls his pilgrim people to join him in his work. This mission culminates in the coming of Christ, the true man, the head of the new humanity, our Lord. He comes to bring shalom, to bring liberty to the captives, sight to the blind, good news to the poor (Isaiah 61:1-4;

97

Luke 4:16-19). It is our Easter faith that he is still alive, providing signs of the fullness of humanity wherever men and women are reconciled to God and to one another. All history moves toward its fulfillment according to God's purpose, and in Jesus Christ we have a foretaste of what that fulfillment will be—a new heaven and a new earth.

Our theological task—laity and clergy together—is to discern the meanings of this pilgrim theology in terms of the way we live and the way we act and the way we shape our ministries in the new age. Here is how one church shaped its thinking as it debated important issues in life.

We believe that God is at work in the world today in many ways and in many places. He actually came into the world in the human form of Jesus Christ as proof of his love for mankind; and through Christ's life, death, and resurrection, we know that his mission in the world will continue until the kingdom is complete. We believe it to be the primary job of the church to seek where God is at work and to follow him there in obedient service.

We believe that God is at work in Burlington [Vermont]. He is in our homes, our places of work, our jail, our courts, our city hall, our slums, our playgrounds, our schools, and our churches. He's at work in urban renewal, reapportionment, race relations, and wherever there is social tension. And, we believe that Christ Church Presbyterian exists in order to join God in his work in Burlington and beyond. To this end, we must boldly set a course of action that will enable us to *be* where he would have us be, and to *do* there what he would have us do.

We believe that parish organization and activity must be consistent with and supportive to this church's purpose. It must be flexible and responsive to the ever-changing location and nature of God's work in the community. And it must be free to change, open to criticism, and willing to fail.

We believe that faithfulness to God is the only criterion by which we can make our decisions.[1]

LAY MISSIONARIES

In "The Missionary Structure of the Congregation"

a clue for a missionary church is provided by the fact that the laity is the bearer of mission. . . . Speaking of the church in terms of laymen means speaking of the church in the world, the church in mission; it means thinking of laymen in terms of their secular competence—in their occupations, their families, their involvement in community affairs and politics. They are to be the bearers of mission in these worldly contexts.[2]

In a society as highly differentiated as our own, we know that unless the layman fulfills his function as a witness there will be vast areas of our life in which no Christian witness is borne. This note has been sounded over and over again in recent years. But we are not at all certain concerning what this means, nor have we yet developed appropriate styles for this witness. It is frustrating to laymen who take seriously the imperative that they are the modern missionaries yet find the translation of that imperative into action tough and tortuous. But for laity who would be faithful there can be no turning away from the task.

The answers are not going to be found until laymen are willing to grasp their share of the responsibility in finding out how to witness in their present world—willing to move beyond stereotypes about witnessing and vague feelings of guilt that somehow it really doesn't come off, to careful training in which the laity and the clergy are partners. The essential style of this training must be the same as the method of witnessing: dialogue. Loren E. Halvorson outlines the meaning of this style:

Monologue is the language of the one who claims to have all the answers.

Dialogue is the language of those who have been broken open and know that they are the ones being questioned.

Monologue is defensive, for it sees its world threatened by questions.

Dialogue is open to all questions. It is persuaded that this is the only way to know the truth.

Monologue is closed, fixed, rigid, dogmatic.

Dialogue is open to the knowledge that one does not possess or control the truth but is possessed by it.

Monologue is the speech of autonomous man who claims to be the center of the universe.

Dialogue is the speech of one who knows he is being addressed by another.

Monologue is the language of the disenchanted, bored, and disillusioned who no longer "listen" to anything.

Dialogue is the language of the adventurer confronting the new with bated breath.

Monologue is the mood of the isolated and lonely masses.

Dialogue expresses the lively chatter within the community of the reconciled.

Monologue fears questions.

Dialogue is exhilarated by quests.

Monologue shapes the truth to fit its own ends. It propagandizes and indoctrinates.

Dialogue involves being shaped by the truth. It is open to new relationships.

Monologue is quick to speak and slow to hear.

Dialogue is quick to hear and slow to speak.

Monologue issues responses quickly in the cheap words of resolutions and prescriptions.

Dialogue answers slowly in deliberate words accompanied by costly deeds.

Monologue remains aloof in the "desert."

Dialogue becomes involved. It enters the city.[3]

Dialogue training for mission is always a two-way street. The laity in their multiplicity of roles make contact with the world. They occupy critical positions and view the world through eyes different from mission; they need theological competence, biblical grounding, and other important help which trained clergy can provide. So clergy and laity need to work together, each contributing to the other, each helping the other perceive the world and the mission, each contributing toward the enlightenment and the enrichment of the other. I urge you laymen to seek training for your task and to understand that this training cannot come in any neat packages but can come only as together with one another and with clergy you ask the right questions and contribute your expertise, dedication, and passion to seeking answers.

PASTORS AS PILGRIMS

Many pastors are really pilgrim men. They are open to the new day which God has given and are taking many risks in helping the churches develop a new style in this changing time. They do not presume to have all the answers, but they are willing to put their life on the line. They need the sympathetic understanding and criticism and cooperation of you laymen. As they stand alongside of you, you need to stand alongside of them.

The profession of the clergy now bears the brunt of the dialogue concerning the structures of the church. Your pastor cannot escape the fact of the changed world. Like you he is a human being—feeling, thinking, reading, responding, changing, and growing. If our culture faces an ethical crisis, a belief crisis, he is no more immune than anyone else. Laymen in the churches need to awaken to this truth.

Many pastors today, especially the younger ones, have come to see that, unless the church is deeply involved in the world and working at solving the critical issues of the age, it is irrelevant. Thus they are busy at work in such areas as civil rights, poverty, and peace. This is disturbing to many lay people. But is this really a new trail they are breaking, or are they only breaking out of the religious ghetto in imitation of him who long ago left Nazareth to go to Jerusalem?

In a thoughtful article in the *Saturday Review*, Theodore C. Sorensen, writing about clergymen who have involved themselves in public issues, has this to say:

> Acting as a churchman instead of a private citizen, he may often find himself in conflict with the views of those to whom he reports. I have no credentials or desire to argue church structure. But I question whether the minister of any church is simply a hired hand, wholly the creature of his superiors or parishioners, wholly bound to accept their dictates and doctrines on matters unrelated to dogma, wholly unable to act in accordance with his own conscience and sense of justice.
>
> To be sure, he should not purport to speak for them. He should not deliberately pressure or embarrass them. But surely there is a 2,000-year-old precedent for a preacher's going beyond good words to good deeds, and then going beyond those good deeds to a direct challenge of both religious and secular authorities, and then going beyond even that direct challenge to enduring imprisonment and violence in order to alter man's ways.
>
> Most men of the cloth, one critic has recently charged, are not competent to deal with such issues. But who among us *is* competent to solve the problems of Vietnam or Watts? The stakes are too great to leave war to the generals, or civil rights to the professionals, or poverty to the social workers. And why should moral battles to right old wrongs, in scriptural fashion, be left to the laymen of the church? Clergymen, like all the rest of us, must learn by doing, by involving themselves in the practical problems of men. The Civil Rights Bill of 1964, according to Senator Russell of Georgia, passed because "those damned preachers had got the idea it was a moral issue." Indeed they had — and indeed it was.[4]

THE STRUCTURE OF THE LOCAL CHURCH

There is much concern about the shape of the Christian mission in a fragmented world. This has arisen not alone because the world has changed but because of important biblical research and theological scholarship. The ensuing debate has caused much anxiety and considerable division in church life, and it is likely to be a storm center for a long time to come. My concern is that instead of trying to solve the problem by dividing up into different camps, stereotyping one another, we work at it with care and devotion as those who have important problems to solve and significant deeds to accomplish together.

We need to see our task first of all as a theological task. Form follows function, the shape of the church's life must emerge from what we believe God is calling us to do. In our pilgrim heritage and in our Protestant history we have important traditions as resources for restructuring. Certainly an important aspect of the Protestant Reformation was a re-formation of church structure.

What we are talking about here is no mere tinkering with the organizational life of the church, no simple social adjustment to changing conditions; we are asking how we can be faithful to God's mission here and now. As familiar as our church structures are and as dear to our hearts as they may be, they are not what gives continuity to the church, but God's mission in the world and his call to us to share in that mission with him.

Pilgrim structures are ad hoc, made for the moment and capable of change in the light of new situations. They are flexible and easy to move—like tents, not like buildings. They are experimental; since it is not always clear where we are going to come out, we must be willing to leave situations open and be willing to fail. When we see the world as a world of constant change, we are on the way to understanding the problems involved in shaping the mission for today and tomorrow; we know this shaping is a continuous process. I recommend, therefore, the establishment in every church of a committee on planning, or a long-range planning committee, or a mission-and-form committee. Whatever we may call it, its task is to take into account, on behalf of the whole church, the changes the church should confront and the need of the local church, in the light of its identity and calling, to shape its life according to the new situation. The rationale for this kind of committee was presented in the previous chapter on planning. The committee should be set up with care. We must take advantage of the broad expertise that exists in almost every church (even the small ones), and at length involve the whole congregation in its work.

Remember, your local church has a ministry to structures as well as to persons. Both functions need to be fulfilled.

We cannot observe the style of Jesus without a deep awareness that his concern was for persons. Therefore, we in our local churches are called to a deep sensitivity to persons. We must be reflective concerning how well we are fulfilling this imperative which God puts upon us: How well are we ministering to persons who are members of our local church? Are those who are baptized and confirmed really on pilgrimage, and do we aid them in their growth and development? What are the operative structures for nurture and assimilation and for equipping for ministry in the world? What is the nature of our relationship to those who are allied to our church but are not members? This is one of the areas of personal evangelism. Do we have any structure for this work to be carried out? In what ways are we serving persons in the community surrounding our church? In what ways are we supporting the wider ministry to persons?

But we have a ministry to structures too. They should be humanized, shaped to the furtherance of truly human ends. This is one of the searing insights that has come to many of us in recent years. As a pastor I sensed deeply that our local church had a ministry to persons; but I operated half blind, for I did poorly in leading my church in a ministry to the structures of society. For example, each Race Relations Sunday a Negro pastor and I exchanged pulpits. My people thought, "How nice to have a Negro pastor in the pulpit!" His people thought, "How nice to have a white pastor in the pulpit!" But nothing changed about our churches in the area of race; our neighborhoods remained the same, and Negroes remained imprisoned in unjust structures. It was not until we perceived the structures of our society as unjust and set out to change them that something that made a difference in the lives of people occurred.

Task force as pilgrim structures. One of the ways we have blocked growth and action in the local church is through the establishment of permanent committees to fulfill certain functions in the life of the church. For example, we have had permanent committees on social action and evangelism. Each of these committees has tended to draw certain kinds of people. Those who want to act but do not pray have tended to become isolated in the social action committee. Those who pray but do not act have been safely corralled in evangelism committees. Both groups have tended to be quite ineffective, and the rest of the church members have rested easy because the agitators in these areas have been safely bottled up, freeing everybody else to forget both functions!

If we are going to face honestly and realistically God's call to us to be for the world, we in the local church are going to have to find the way to let those who want to shape their lives around the needs of the world, and who see the local church as an important means to this end, become free to influence the shape of the life of the church. Most people think of the old-line Protestant churches as broad churches. Actually they are not, for they are structured to favor talk instead of action. If we are going to take seriously our ministry to persons and structures, in both social action and evangelism, we must find a way of unfreezing the present situation. The clue is that evangelism and social action are bound inextricably together, and the local church exists for a mission that includes both. The task force as a pilgrim structure may be an important means of our turning more fully toward the world today as we seek to fulfill this mission. Here are some guidelines for such a group.

The task force is formed in response to a particular issue or function. Those interested and willing to act in that field come together for careful study of the problem, with the understanding that after it has been studied, decision will be made and action taken.

Task forces may be formed around all the significant issues confronted by the congregation in the public and residential world. They may range from task forces on personal evangelism, stewardship, and Christian education to such issues as the struggle for racial justice, ministry to the dispossessed and disenfranchised, the urban revolution, ethical problems emerging from the scientific-technological revolution, and the problems of peace.

Task forces should not be confused with study groups. The study-group movement has been one of the vital movements in the life of the church in our time, and we cannot carry on the mission without study. But we must accept the fact that many of the study groups in the church have become cozy nooks where important human issues are glossed over and from which no significant action eventuates. Task groups are also study and research groups, but they differ in that they aim at hard decisions and action. Task groups proceed on the basis of the isolation of the human problem; careful study of that problem in the light of the Scriptures; decision, action, and evaluation; and new action in the light of the evaluation.

Task groups may be appointed by an official body of the church and as such be responsible to that body, or they may form as ad hoc structures without official authorization. When the latter is the case, a task force does not act in the name of the church. It gladly testifies to what it has learned; individual witness is made; but care is taken not to speak for the particular local church. The group is always willing to meet with and join in action with all who share their concern, be they Christian or non-Christian—and with other groups, be they church or nonchurch.

Task groups go out of existence when they have fulfilled their intended function or when that function is assumed elsewhere.

The academy methodology as a pilgrim style. The European academies provide another effective means of addressing the human problem as men of faith. There are forty-six of these academies in full operation in Europe. Several years ago it was my privilege to study the work of many of them, to participate in conferences with miners, teachers, military personnel, industrial heads, labor leaders, apprentices, a cross section of a whole factory, and many others. In seeking to isolate the methodology of these academies, this is what I found.

The questions discussed in the academies are not the inside questions of the church; they are the secular questions of the man in the world.

The church in these conversations does not take a superior position, speaking vertically; its position is that of "alongsidedness," on the horizontal level.

The specialist from the world speaks to the problems of the man in the street, and the theologian as one of the specialists takes his place among other specialists.

Conferees who have given up the church or are outright atheists exceed in number those who have a warm, intimate relationship with the church. This should not frighten or discourage us. We cannot speak to the world unless we listen; we cannot bring good tidings unless we go to the ones we hope will listen.

Roman Catholics, Protestants, Jews, and people of other religions and of no religion gather together in the conferences around the questions of the man in the world.

The essential methodology is that of a dialogue taking place within the context of addressing the questions being shaped in formal lectures by specialists.

No visible attempt is made to capitalize on the situation for the church or to pressure people into a particular point of view or action. Worship is offered, but optional, at all the conferences.

All the academies try to talk with a person within the context of his vocation, knowing that an important decision-making dimension of his life centers there. Some of the academies specialize in a particular vocation.

A number of academies are especially related to industry, working with labor leaders and industrial heads and within particular professional groupings.

In these conferences, the gospel is proclaimed and sometimes heard.

These principles are sound. The academy movement has proved itself to be a significant model of mission in the world, and there is no good reason to wait before putting this methodology into operation on this side of the Atlantic. Of course we cannot depend solely on new institutions. We need also a new stance on the part of the churches already in our communities. Nor do I wish to convey the idea that many of these principles are not already in operation here and there in America. But in our ecumenical age the time is ripe for this methodology to come into full flowering in thousands of communities across the country. I hope that much experimentation will be done in and between local churches.

We cannot determine what shape this academy methodology will take in America. Certainly we cannot merely transplant what the Europeans have done. For our distinctive situation we have to develop our own style. However, certain characteristics will be found in each situation.

American academies will be ecumenical. All the religious groups in a community may not join, but all would be welcome and invited.

Conferences will be led not on the church's questions but on the questions of the man in the street.

The church will be present as a peer in the form of laity, pastors, and theologians—but the church will be present only as a peer.

The theologian will join with other specialists in addressing the problem or problems. He will be in dialogue—really listening and speaking—open to changes the other person may convince him of.

Task forces will be related to the issue addressed.

If we adapt these principles to our own needs, the church will find a way to fulfill its function of participating responsibly in a dialogue with the world. By looking carefully at the issues of ethics and politics, the church will help men in their struggle toward meaning and value in this new age.

PILGRIM CELEBRATION

The local church as the pilgrim people of God exists as a community of memory and hope. We remember what God has done in his mighty acts; we remember that our Lord Jesus Christ is at work in his world and is calling us to follow him. Our worship is our celebration of the mighty acts of God as they become for us living, compelling, contemporary realities.

Worship is essentially celebration, a lifting up and rejoicing in what binds us together, our faith and our hope. But oftentimes our worship is dull and thin because we have been a community of amnesia and nostalgia, not a community of living memory and hope; and we have often acted as though God were dead and as though there were little relationship between our daily life, the great issues of the world, and what goes on Sunday morning. The gap between God's mission and the local church has grown too broad. So, while we are busy in our churches thinking about the age that is new and the many crises that are upon us, let us add one more deep concern—the crisis in worship.

Can our encounter with the living God be more real if our style of worship becomes more dialogic? Some pastors hold talk-back sessions after morning worship. Some allow task-force reporting as part of the worship. Other possibilities only await the freeing of our imagination under the direction of the Spirit. Are we willing to risk greater flexibility in our worship, allowing in each worship some time when anything can happen? Can we dramatize our relationship to the world in a more real fashion? Some churches now have the reading of important articles from the newspaper before the morning prayer. As we think and plan in this area, perhaps our primary criteria ought to be the bringing together of our communion with God and participation in his mission.

Chapter **8**

Hope in Action

WHEN I AM homeward bound from a field assignment, I am usually very tired. I have been with people for days, talked and listened for days. More talk and listening is not exactly what I need. When my seat mate on the plane is chatty, I have a surefire way of turning him off. When he asks me what I do for a living, I say, "I work in the field of evangelism." The conversation is over. The word evangelism has frightened him, for he fears I am going to grasp him by the lapel and ask, "Brother, are you saved?" Or he suspects that I may take a tape recorder out of my brief-case and force him to listen! Or he is just nervous because he is sitting next to a religious fanatic. The rest of the trip he will stick with his magazine.

When I am outward bound to a field trip, I am not tired and am open to conversation. Then, when my seat mate asks me what I do for a living, I tell him, "I am a church executive convinced that we live in a new age, and my task is to help the church adjust her mental and institutional structures to serve appropriately under these new conditions. I'm concerned about the meaning of existence, change, and conflict, the new morality, the new theology, hungry people, overpopulation, war and peace, city planning, and the church's relationship to all these problems." A lively conversation has begun. Before the plane lands I have heard important things and have had a chance to witness to some things that are alive in me.

Though the word evangelism has not been used, it is what this book is about. Evangelism is a crucial dimension of the church's life, but the word itself is the symbol of the complexity of our task and the current confusion of tongues. Some of the most important words in the Christian vocabulary no longer communicate what we intend; some communicate nothing at all. The word evangelism today fails to express its full-orbed meaning, the communication of good news. But the responsibility to which the word points is clear—the task of speaking and being good news in the world.

WHAT EVANGELISM IS NOT

Evangelism is not a high-pressure way of "selling Christianity." It is not a take-it-or-leave-it pious monologue. It is not a high- or low-pressure means of getting more church members. It is not slick propaganda for Jesus. It is not a clever way to make our churches bigger and better, increasing their security and success. Evangelism is not overpowering another person and forcing him to listen, or manipulating him in order to get him to think what you want him to think or to accept your system. It is not a one-way-street conversation in which the evangelist gives the answer while the sinner holds still.

114

WHAT EVANGELISM IS

It is being truly present to another person, being there in the deepest sense of the term, knowing that God is present to you both, as present as each will permit.

It is listening, open-ended listening, prayerfully trying to understand what the other person is saying through his words and feelings.

It is being an overflowing bucket, in the midst of the dialogue telling what cannot be kept in—good news!

It is telling our story, the story of a pilgrim people, supremely the story of Jesus Christ, God's true man and true hope.

It is speaking from the bottom of the heart, not from the top of the head.

It is speaking more to the heart than to the head.

It is inviting others to a pilgrimage in discipleship to Jesus Christ.

It is the sharing and celebrating of beauty, truth, goodness, and love.

It is a joyful throwing of your faith into the air.

It is a healing word spoken and a healing deed done.

It is an act of reconciliation.

It is a cup of cold water given.

It is a life lived authentically and humbly.

It is a hope shared—a hope for this neighbor and every neighbor.

I have been speaking of personal evangelism. Beyond person-to-person encounter is encounter between institutions and persons and between institutions and institutions —all this is done in the name of Jesus Christ to make and keep life truly human—all that acts out and speaks of the life of Jesus Christ in and for our own time. Evangelism is all that we do to communicate what God has done and is doing for the world in Jesus Christ.

THE COMPLEXITY OF COMMUNICATION

We church members must look steadily at the church in the midst of an emerging new age. We know that it would be less painful to look either at the church or at the emerging new age—less painful than to keep one eye on each. The problems and complexities of life which affect the life of the church affect the problem of the communication of the gospel in this new world.

The church must learn by listening and experimenting. But the church is not called simply to embrace the new age. It is not called merely to reverse the monologue—listening now, instead of speaking. As the pilgrim people of God we speak out of a rich tradition of the God revealed to us through the world of the Bible. But we know that we have the responsibility of speaking of God in the language of *this* day, *today.* Just as Luther translated the Bible into the common speech of his day, we have to speak in the modern idiom—otherwise we cannot be heard. Notice I say "cannot": it is not that the world obstinately refuses to hear archaic speech; it is that the world is unable to understand our fathers' "language of Zion."

We must dare to speak of God to a pragmatic, critical age that scorns the supernatural. We must struggle to speak of him even while we are convinced that we need a massive restatement of the gospel in a time when many traditional symbols such as heaven and hell have lost their power to illumine and move men.

We are in a wilderness phase in evangelism, a time of testing, of reshaping, a time when we do not know precisely how to speak so that modern man will hear our message.

116

The pilgrim motif applies to evangelism today. This book is about *pilgrim evangelism.*

ENCOUNTER WITH GOD

"Now the Lord said to Abram, 'Go. . . .' " As a pilgrim people of God he still comes to us in the Haran of our personal existence and in our corporate life as a people, and he says, "Go. . . ." A new age stretches out ahead of us, a future mysterious and threatening, hopeful and fearful. Haran is our familiar territory. Here, we think, is safety, and we want to stay where we are. But always the future opens up and our God bids us enter with more faith than fear.

We encounter this God of Abraham, this pilgrim God, in Jesus Christ our Lord. As the United Church of Christ Statement of Faith puts it, "In Jesus Christ, the man of Nazareth, . . . he has come to us and shared our common lot, conquering sin and death and reconciling the world to himself." We believe that this Jesus is the hope of the whole world and that his presence is transforming the world, redirecting it to its promised end. He is the worldly Christ, set loose in the events and movements of our time. It is he who gives meaning to our life, and it is his story that has shaped our history.

In this new time evangelism is what it always has been —a call to man to acknowledge Jesus Christ as the Lord of life. This is not a lordship removed from everyday existence, nor is it a narrow lordship over some special area of pious religious practice. In this new day we see with clarity that personal religion and religion concerned with the world cannot be separated: Jesus has torn down the wall dividing the sacred and the secular and the wall dividing the individual and the collective. "Jesus is Lord" was the earliest Christian confession and the seed of all creeds. To

117

live it in our present world requires a new involvement in the living issues of the world and a new understanding of faithfulness.

Does it not then become clear that when we decide to be for Jesus Christ we must also decide to be with him in his work of bringing shalom—justice, peace, freedom—to the world? Not the acceptance of a system, but a changed life! Not a decision to be a member of an institution, but a decision to live out the life of Christ among men in the structures of the world! This is God's mission. Evangelism is the call to participate in it.

When I talk of pilgrim evangelism I speak of conversion in the deeply and broadly biblical sense. In "The Missionary Structure of the Congregation" studies we find these words:

Traditional evangelism emphasized conversion mainly as a movement of turning away from the world. There is biblical ground for such an emphasis in that conversion always involves renunciation of attitudes based on self-interest. But the biblical view of conversion envisages a double movement, the turning away from preoccupation with one's own interest and the turning toward the interests of the neighbor (Philippians 2:3). It is a movement of turning away from the world in that the terms of the world, based on self-interest, can no longer be accepted. At the same time it is a turning *toward* the world, now seen from the perspective of hope, in the light of God's purpose.

If conversion involves turning to the world in hope, participation in God's mission becomes a movement reaching out into the future whose outcome cannot be predicted. The one-sided emphasis on conversion in traditional evangelism has tended to presuppose a predictable outcome such as joining a church and beginning to think and act as a church member. In pursuing this goal, evangelism has become a form of proselytism, a call on the part of insiders to outsiders inviting them to come into the inside. However, in conversion something new happens to both the outsider and the insider. For conversion ultimately is God's work, who through his spirit creates a new situation. It is a movement toward the world into which both insider and outsider are called jointly to enter and in which they together become participants in God's mission.[1]

VISION

"By faith Abraham obeyed when he was called to go out to a place which he was to receive as an inheritance" (Heb. 11:8). Good news for man today comes in terms of a vision of tomorrow. Our task in the new age is to offer our vision to the world. This vision comes to us out of the ages and out of our age, as Abraham's vision came to him out of his encounter with God. What a vision it is, the vision of shalom, a new heaven and a new earth, Jerusalem, the kingdom of God!

We live in a day of great vision. The nations are stirring, new hopes emerge for people long held in colonial and racial captivity. Talk with them of the vision of tomorrow and you have instant attention. But is it not a tragedy that so much of the vision that belongs to us as a pilgrim people is clouded with thick tradition, antique notions, moth-eaten hymns, and pious language? It needs to be translated into contemporary human terms that will again cause a leap of joy in the hearts of men. Our Christian vision is hidden in the concept of shalom, in Jesus Christ who incarnates this vision, and in our belief that our Lord is at work in the world, setting man free to be man.

OPENNESS TO THE FUTURE

"[Abraham] went out, not knowing where he was to go. By faith he sojourned in the land of promise, as in a foreign land" (Heb. 11:8-9). One aspect of our evangelistic task is to translate the promises of God and the vision deriving from them into contemporary language and hopes. What, for example, is the relation of this biblical passage to Ephesians and the emergence of global man: "For he has made

119

known to us in all wisdom and insight the mystery of his will, according to his purpose which he set forth in Christ as a plan for the fullness of time, to unite all things in him, things in heaven and things on earth" (Eph. 1:9-10)?

We live in a pluralistic age. Christendom no longer calls the shots. The day of global man is here. The new mobility with its heavy pressures toward openness breaks down dividing walls. We dare not shrink from the new meanings and values in these revolutionary developments. They throw into crisis our mental and institutional structures. We must find out why, and make appropriate responses.

The pilgrim style of openness to the future must lead us to a new openness to research and experimentation in the life of the church and to the courage to use the findings responsibly. "The Missionary Structure of the Congregation" studies have defined six motifs that act as divining rods of God's action or as clues that alert us as to how God is moving in his work of redemption today. George Younger, in an important unpublished paper, suggests, "We must be prepared to research all of these hypotheses about missionary action as well as any others that we have inherited from the past or can imagine for the future." [2] The six clues are:

1. *God/world/church.* God's object of concern is the world, and the church is that part of the world where this concern is recognized and celebrated.

2. *History and self-understanding.* The world can only be understood historically, as part of the transaction between God and the world. Men are involved in this historical process and called upon to assume responsibility as partners with God.

3. *Participation in God's mission.* The missionary call is a call for participation with God in his redemptive work in creation.

120

4. *Humanization.* Christ provides signs of the fullness of humanity, wherever men and women are led to restored relationships.

5. *Laity—the reference group for mission.* A servant church conducts its mission in the world through the corporate ministry of the laity.

6. *Pluriformity of structures.* In a pluriform world the Christian community will act through at least four types of structures: family-type; permanent availability; permanent community; task force.[3]

"LIVING IN TENTS"—FLEXIBLE STRUCTURES

Good news is not communicated by means of tradition-encrusted, overdeveloped systems and institutions. Boredom soon comes and a tired yawn is the only response modern man will make to our tiresome arguments hooked into an age that is gone. The new age threatens these arguments and makes them largely irrelevant. Thus, Monica Furlong says: "While the holocaust is sweeping away much that is beautiful and all that is safe and comfortable and unquestioned, it is relieving us of mounds of Christian bric-a-brac, and the liberation is unspeakable." [4]

Mental structures as well as institutional structures must be flexible in pilgrim theology. We must "go native" in language and forms if we hope to communicate the gospel today. Though we are making some progress in language and some in forms, the hardest work remains to be done. Many church members are aware that one of the most obsolete forms of Christian social existence is denominationalism. Old sectarian divisions are seen to be dysfunctional and will have to be replaced. They get in the way of modern man's hearing and responding to the message and in many ways cancel the message. Denominationalism hangs around the neck of today's church like an albatross.

121

We must sense that the ancient truths that inform our life as a pilgrim people of God will have to be clothed in a contemporary idiom. The Anglican theologian Harry Williams says: "If to the seeker after Christ you preach a fourth-century Christ or a sixteenth-century Christ or a nineteenth-century Christ, you are still giving him a stone instead of the living truth." [5] In the phrase "the man for others," Bonhoeffer has given the primary clue of the contemporary Christ.

THE CHURCH FOR OTHERS

As Christians and as the Christian church, our calling is to follow the example of Jesus Christ as suffering Servant and risen Lord. Our task is to be concerned for man as Jesus was concerned, to be truly present for the neighbor, and to be present in answering his question "How can I find a gracious neighbor?"

Industrial-missioner Horst Symanowski says:

The question of previous ages, such as Luther's question when he was in and even after he left the monastery: "How can I find a gracious God?"—this was the question that drove men to search desperately for an answer. It was the motor of their behavior in the world, unleashed crusades, and started wars. It drove men and wouldn't let them sleep. But how many people today are awakened to rise and seek answers to this question? Most of us sleep on it pretty well. Either we don't ask it, or it appears to us as a mere historical, antiquated question. But another question does drive us around . . . agitates whole people, and forces us into anxiety and despair: "How can I find a gracious neighbor?" How can we still (somehow) live together? Man and wife, superiors and subordinates, colleagues in competitive struggle, and finally one people with another, East and West? Here we become excited, ask questions, and seek ways. The question of a gracious neighbor has become the cardinal question of our industrial society.[6]

122

A most important clue is found in Luke 15, in Jesus' familiar parables of the lost sheep, the lost coin, and the lost son. The sheep is lost because of his aimlessness; the coin is lost because of another's fault; the son is lost because of his willfulness. The sheep is found by the shepherd because he is willing to risk the loss of the ninety and nine; the coin is found by dogged persistence; the son is saved by compassion, the love-power to enter redemptively into the suffering of another. Important ideas for God's pilgrim people in this time of pilgrim evangelism! We cannot be there for others, present to persons one at a time, without grave risk. We cannot bring good news except by persistence. And, unless we are willing to enter into the suffering of persons one at a time and all at once, our good news will turn to ashes on our tongues.

FAITH AND HOPE

"By faith Abraham obeyed when he was called. . . . He looked forward to the city which has foundations, whose builder and maker is God" (Heb. 11:8, 10). Faith trusts in God's promises. As the pilgrim people of God we know that our participation in God's mission is a matter of faith, and this faith is hope in action.

To be a "missionary" is to risk one's hope in challenging man in this world. Mission is hope in action, not merely a missionary in action. Mission is not defined by an individual Christian or a Christian community going somewhere or doing something. Mission is defined only by our hope that God will have the last word in this world. This hope must be concretely worked out amidst the manifold temptations to abandon it as hopeless.[7]

There is a painting by G. F. Watts depicting hope as a woman with a bandage over her eyes, sitting bowed in an empty universe, trying to make music on one string of a broken lyre. A much better image of hope for us today is that of the disciples after the resurrection. They knew that because of the coming of Jesus Christ their lives were changed, and not only their lives but the whole world. They moved with courage and confidence not because they saw clearly the road before them but because of their hope that the risen Lord preceded them into the future.

It is this spirit that must infuse the church which now is at the end of one age and the beginning of another. The way ahead is not sharply etched; we glimpse only dimly the dangers that lie in the path of our pilgrim feet. But as a people who long ago followed a cloud by day and a pillar of fire by night, we press on in faith and hope, confident that he who calls us and is with us now will be with us to the end of time. As our Christian hope becomes enfleshed in word and peace, we shall speak and be good news in an age that, while new, is still burdened with history's bad news.

And out of our family history, out of the long ago, there comes to us the warning of Lot's wife, who "looked back, and she became a pillar of salt" (Gen. 19:26).

Notes

Chapter 1

1. Colin Williams, *Faith in a Secular Age* (New York: Harper & Row, 1966), p. 36.
2. Dietrich Bonhoeffer, *Prisoner for God: Letters and Papers from Prison* (New York: Macmillan, 1961), pp. 168-69.
3. J. C. Hoekendijk, *The Church Inside Out,* trans. Isaac C. Rottenberg (Philadelphia: Westminster Press, 1966), p. 21. Copyright © J. C. Hoekendijk, 1964. English trans. copyright © 1966, by W. L. Jenkins. Used by permission.

Chapter 2

1. Marshall W. Fishwick, " 'Everything Nailed Down Is Coming Loose,' " *Saturday Review,* June 29, 1963, p. 11.
2. Walter W. Sikes, "The Great New Fact of Our Time," *Revolution and Renewal: Christian Response to the Technological and Social Revolutions of Our Time,* Study Book for Churches in the United States in Preparation for a World Conference on Church and Society (Indianapolis: Commission on Church and Society of the Christian Churches, 1965), p. 2.
3. Harold K. Schilling, "On Religion and Science Making Common Cause," unpublished paper.
4. "Cybernetics," a word coined by Norbert Wiener, refers to the computer governing of production and services through data processing. Systems of two-way automated control (with feedback) "pilot" the process; thus the use of the Greek word for "pilot, steersman, governor."
5. Donald N. Michael, *Cybernation: The Silent Conquest* (Santa Barbara: Center for the Study of Democratic Institutions, 1962), pp. 6, 13-14.

6. William D. Smith, "Computers: Instruments for Change," *The New York Times,* Jan. 9, 1967.

7. *Ibid.*

8. Harold C. Letts, "Abstract of Our Changing World," unpublished paper.

9. Quoted by Robert Theobald, "The Economic and Social Impact of Cybernetics: Problems of Social Reorganization," an address given at the Conference on Cybernetics and Society, Georgetown University, Nov. 19, 1964.

10. *Ibid.*

11. *Ibid.*

12. Sikes, *op. cit.,* p. 6.

13. Donald Michael, "Forces and Trends Pointing to the Future: The Next Twenty Years," unpublished paper.

14. Lynton K. Caldwell, "Biopolitics: Science, Ethics, and Public Policy," *Yale Review,* LVI, No. 8 (Oct., 1964), 8. Copyright Yale University.

15. National Council of Churches Information Service, Feb. 13, 1965, summarizes the WHO study.

16. Harvey Cox, *The Secular City* (New York: Macmillan, 1965), p. 2.

Chapter 3

1. See "Education in Our Changing World" by Huston Smith, professor of philosophy, Massachusetts Institute of Technology —a lecture at the Consultation on Continuing Education for the Ministry, Andover Newton Theological School, June 15-18, 1964.

2. Harriet B. Kurtz, War Control Planners, Inc., Box 35, Chappaqua, N.Y. 10514.

3. Harold K. Schilling, *Science and Religion* (New York: Charles Scribner's Sons, 1962).

4. Harold K. Schilling, "On Religion and Science Making Common Cause," unpublished paper.

5. *Ibid.*

6. Erik H. Erikson, *Childhood and Society* (New York: W. W. Norton & Co., 1950).

7. See Herman F. Reissig, *Man's New Home* (Philadelphia: United Church Press, 1964).

Chapter 5

1. *The Church for Others and the Church for the World: A Quest for Structures for Missionary Congregations,* Final Re-

port of the Western Working Group and North American Working Group of the Department on Studies in Evangelism (Geneva, Switzerland: World Council of Churches, 1967). See also *Planning for Mission,* ed. Thomas Wieser (New York: The U.S. Conference for the World Council of Churches, 1966).

2. *Planning for Mission,* pp. 70-71.

Chapter 6

1. Perry L. Norton, *Church and Metropolis* (New York: Seabury Press, 1964), p. 49.

Chapter 7

1. "The Church for the World," Report of the North American Working Group, "The Missionary Structure of the Congregation," Study Sponsored by the World Council of Churches, Part IV, p. 4.
2. *Ibid.,* Part II, p. 12.
3. Loren E. Halvorson, *Exodus into the World* (Tower Book; Minneapolis: Augsburg, 1966), pp. 53-54. Reprinted by permission of Augsburg Publishing House, Minneapolis, Minn., copyright owners.
4. Theodore C. Sorensen, "New and Future Clergy," *Saturday Review,* April 30, 1966, p. 24.

Chapter 8

1. "The Church for the World," Report of the North American Working Group, "The Missionary Structure of the Congregation," Study Sponsored by the World Council of Churches, Part II, pp. 7-8.
2. George Younger, "Action Research and Evaluation in Mission," unpublished paper.
3. See "The Church for the World," Part II.
4. Monica Furlong, *Time* magazine, Dec. 25, 1964, p. 46.
5. *Ibid.,* p. 47.
6. Horst Symanowski, *The Christian Witness in an Industrial Society,* trans. George H. Kehm (Philadelphia: Westminster Press, 1964), p. 50. Copyright © 1964, W. L. Jenkins. Used by permission.
7. *Planning for Mission,* ed. Thomas Wieser (New York: The U.S. Conference for the World Council of Churches, 1966), p. 34.